T0353920

DON'T WORRY

48 Lessons on Achieving Calm

SHUNMYŌ MASUNO

Illustrated by Zanna and Harry Goldhawk

Translated by Allison Markin Powell

MICHAEL JOSEPH

Shunmyō Masuno, the head priest of a 450-year-old
Zen Buddhist temple in Japan, is the author of the
international bestseller *The Art of Simple Living* as well as
being an award-winning Zen garden designer for clients all
over the world and a professor of environmental design at
one of Japan's leading art schools. He has lectured widely,
including at the Harvard Graduate School of Design, Cornell
University and Brown University.

Contents

FOREWORD

PART ONE

Reduce, let go, leave behind

The Zen way of keeping anxiety and worry at bay

1. Don't delude yourself   14

2. Focus on 'now'   18

3. Don't burden yourself or drag yourself down   22

4. Pare down your belongings   26

5. Just be, as you are   30

6. Take off your coloured glasses   34

7. Be gracious   39

8. Recognize limitations   42

PART TWO

Concentrate only on things you can achieve here and now
By doing so, you'll stop thinking about unnecessary things

9.	Reconsider the obvious	*48*
10.	Don't rush, don't panic	*51*
11.	Respond positively	*55*
12.	Cherish the morning	*60*
13.	Live by your own standards	*65*
14.	Don't seek out the unnecessary	*69*
15.	Shine wherever you find yourself	*73*
16.	Don't go against your feelings	*77*
17.	Make your evenings calm	*81*

PART THREE

Step away from competition and things will fall into place

'People are people, and I am who I am'

18.	Don't fixate on victory or defeat	86
19.	Keep at it, slow and steady	90
20.	Experience gratitude	93
21.	Use the right words	97
22.	Let young people take charge	100
23.	Accept your circumstances, whatever they may be	103
24.	Do today's things today	107
25.	Don't simply run away	111
26.	Be more tolerant	114
27.	Go with the flow	118
28.	Don't just talk for the sake of talking	122
29.	Adjust your breathing	126
30.	Change the 'air' in your home	130

PART FOUR

Surprising tips for improving relationships
How to form good connections and let go of bad ones

31. Cherish your connections   *136*

32. Make good connections   *140*

33. Yield to others   *144*

34. Don't wield 'logic'   *148*

35. Spend ten minutes a day in nature   *152*

36. Make people want to see you again   *156*

37. Admit errors right away   *160*

38. Don't hesitate to ask for help   *164*

39. Be a good listener   *166*

40. Don't base decisions on profits and losses   *170*

PART FIVE

Change *how* you worry about things and your life
will change for the better
On money, aging, illness, death, and more

41.	Money	*176*
42.	Getting Older	*180*
43.	Old Age	*183*
44.	Love	*185*
45.	Marriage	*188*
46.	Children	*192*
47.	Death	*196*
48.	One's End	*200*

foreword

PARE AWAY THE THINGS YOU DON'T NEED.
LIVE AN INFINITELY SIMPLE LIFE FREE FROM
UNNECESSARY ANXIETY OR WORRY, WITHOUT
BEING SWAYED BY OTHER PEOPLE'S VALUES

— — — — —

I hope to tell you how to do that in this book.

By nature of being a Zen Buddhist priest, I am consulted by many people about their problems. The variety of what they want to talk about is endless, but if I were to generalize, I would classify them as anxieties, worries and doubts.

When I listen carefully to these concerns, here is what I notice: almost all of them are in fact delusions, assumptions, mistaken impressions, or imaginary fears. You might even say they lack any substance.

'How can you be so dismissive,' someone might say to me, 'when you're not the one going through it?' Or, 'I'm so worried about it that I can't eat!'

It's a little like a Japanese saying about seeing a ghost out in the field when it's really just dried susuki grasses. What I mean is, there's no reason to be afraid of what might appear to be a ghost,

because it's really nothing more than withered stalks. These things that tie us into knots and drag down our spirits are no different. The truth is, if we look at them objectively, we find that we often allow ourselves to fear shadows that aren't really there.

Maybe this sounds familiar: something you were worried about was weighing you down, but then a random comment or occurrence made you realize how insignificant it was and you were amazed by how much lighter you felt . . .

Zen teachings are a treasure trove for this kind of realization.

I wonder what you think of when you hear the word 'Zen'. Perhaps it conjures an esoteric world of lofty and profound ideas. It's true: we do sometimes engage in abstract conversations about Zen koans. But this is misleading.

Zen teachings can be very accessible.

They are closely connected to our everyday lives.

For example, when you enter a home and take off your shoes, line them up neatly. Even something as simple as this is rooted in Zen: it is a literal reflection of the Zen saying, 'Look carefully at what is under your own feet.'

In Zen we use phrases and sayings called zengo as part of our training. Zengo derive from anecdotes and scriptures to help us understand the wisdom and practice of Zen. You'll find them throughout this book, and collected at the end in an index.

Another zengo, 'Eat and drink with your whole heart,' teaches us not to be distracted by unnecessary things. When you drink a cup of tea, focus only on drinking the tea, or when you eat a meal, focus only on eating that meal.

This might all seem perfectly ordinary, but if we take great care to put these habits into practice, we will be able to focus on the here and now. By doing so, we will free ourselves from unnecessary anxiety, and our mind will be able to settle.

So, instead of agonizing over what might happen in the future, let's focus only on the here and now. The point is to reduce, to let go, to leave behind . . . By doing so, we'll be able to enjoy a calmer, more relaxed and positive version of our selves.

Gasshō
SHUNMYŌ MASUNO

part one

Reduce, let go, leave behind

The Zen way of keeping anxiety and worry at bay

1. DON'T DELUDE YOURSELF

Zen teaches us not to compare ourselves

There is a zengo, or Zen saying, 'Delude not thyself.'

Put more plainly, it means 'do not have delusions.'

You might think that delusions refer to any number of figments of the imagination.

But in Zen, the concept of delusion has a much deeper and broader meaning.

Whatever lodges in your mind, that clings to and constrains your heart – these are all delusions.

Selfish desires for this or that, attachments that we don't want to let go of – these too are delusions.

Envy of others, feelings of self-doubt – these are also delusions.

Of course, it's impossible to free ourselves of every delusion that takes hold in our minds. That is the state that the Buddha achieved. Being human, we must accept that there will always be delusions in our hearts and minds.

The important thing is to reduce these delusions, as much as we can. We're all capable of it. But in order to do so, we must first discern the true character of our delusions.

There is a famous quote from Sun Tzu, 'Know your enemy, know thyself, and you shall not fear a hundred battles.' Which is to say, without knowing your enemy, you will not understand what you must do in order to face him.

What is the source of these delusions?

It is a way of thinking that sees things in opposition.

For example, we set up binaries such as life and death, winning and losing, beauty and ugliness, rich and poor, profit and loss, love and hate.

Death is seen as being in conflict with life, and when the two are compared, we perceive life as sacred and precious, while death is empty and forlorn.

'That guy's lucky. I never seem to catch a break.'

'How come I lose at everything, while she's always winning?'

A single experience bleeds into everything. We apply this to our whole lives. Meanwhile, envy of others and feelings of self-condemnation build up inside us until we are consumed by them.

Indeed, one could say that we are under the sway of those around us, that we are bound by our delusions.

But ask yourself this: what meaning is found in comparing yourself with others?

There is a zengo, 'Once enlightened, there are no favourites.'

If we apply this to human relationships, perhaps we can accept others as they are, regardless of whether we like them or hate them (or whether they are better or worse than we are), without being carried away by our emotions.

The founder of the Soto school of Zen Buddhism, Dogen Zenji, said, 'The actions of others are not my own.' He taught that what others do is unrelated to what we do ourselves. Someone else's efforts do not lead to our advancement. The only way for us to improve is through our own efforts.

Zen teaches that the existence of every thing and every person is absolute, unto itself – there is no comparison.

This is true for you, and true for others.

There is no comparison. When we attempt to compare things for which there is no comparison, we become preoccupied by what is irrelevant, and this is what creates anxiety, worry and fear.

When you stop comparing, you'll see that 90 per cent of your delusions disappear. Your heart feels lighter. Life is more relaxed.

'Don't delude yourself' – think of these words every so often. Let them become a way to cheer yourself on, to say, 'I believe in my absolute self, without compare!'

2. FOCUS ON 'NOW'

This is about cherishing ourselves

— — — — —

Some people brood over memories. You might say they are stuck in the past.

There is a zengo, 'Dwell in the breath.'

Taken literally, it means to live in the moment when you are drawing breath, as conscientiously as you possibly can.

This also resonates with the Buddhist concept 'Dwell in the three worlds.'

The three worlds are the past, the present and the future. We live in the connections among these three worlds, though when we find ourselves in the present, the past is already dead while the future is about to be born.

This is how we explain the Buddhist concept of samsara, the cycle of death and rebirth – how everything is born and then dies, and everything that dies is reborn.

Put another way, there's no use rethinking the past that is dead and gone, nor should we think about the future that has yet to be born until it arrives.

That is to say, all that matters is how we live in the here and now.

There is this three-line poem, known as a senryu:

Even the chipped bowl
Was once a cherry tree
On Mount Yoshino

What now appears to be a worn-out piece of china was once a magnificent cherry tree in full bloom on Mount Yoshino, where throngs of onlookers gasped in wonder at its beauty.

Our past glory and honour become the foundation for our present state.

But this is not only about Yoshino cherry blossoms. Some people seem never to miss a chance to bring up their brilliant past.

'I worked on such a huge job.'

'I'm the one who made that project a success.'

Of course, it's important to acknowledge the satisfaction one feels about a job well-done. It's also nice to raise a glass to celebrate a victory.

But is it appropriate to linger so often on old stories? Let's shift our perspective a bit.

'Not that old hobby horse again. It's so tedious and boring.'

Have you ever heard something like that?

Quite honestly, it's unpleasant to have to listen, over and over again, to long-winded tales of past glories. And isn't it rather unseemly for the one doing the talking? It's hard not to think that they are quite unhappy.

A fixation on the past is an indication of a person's lack of confidence in the present. This is how anxiety, worry and fear creep into your heart and mind.

One might even say it's equivalent to undermining your present self.

I'll reiterate this so it will be etched into your mind: all that matters is how we live in the here and now.

If you bemoan the fact that your present self is nothing more than a chipped bowl (or a dead-end job . . .), that will only magnify your unhappiness. Even a chipped bowl can be a vessel for delicious soup to warm someone's soul.

Now let's be the best chipped bowl we can be!

To me, that's what it means to dwell in the breath.

3. DON'T BURDEN YOURSELF
OR DRAG YOURSELF DOWN

Create a spot in your living space where your spirit can settle

— · — · — · — —

Do you have a 'spiritual abode'?

At one time, almost every Japanese home had an altar
or a shrine.

It was a natural everyday occurrence to see each family
member sitting before it, offering incense (if it was a Buddhist
altar) and then putting their hands together.

Children learned the practice from watching their parents and
grandparents – hands clasped in prayer and worship – and
at the same time, it also nurtured reverence for one's ancestors.

Perhaps you agree that this is one of Japan's fine traditions,
a beautiful custom.

Back in the day, when another branch of the family would set
up house, one of the first things they would do was put up an
altar and welcome their ancestors into the new home. For this
reason, altars were to be found in every house, and ancestors
were present in each family's everyday lives.

But nowadays, how many people have an altar in their home? If we're counting only people who live in cities, that number is most likely extremely low. Whereas surely the housing situation is one factor, there is a bigger reason.

And that has to do with the fact that an overwhelming majority of city dwellers settled there after the war, leaving their hometowns at a young age to move to urban centres. In these people's minds, their ancestors remained back in their hometown, protecting their parents or the head of the family, and so they themselves did not feel that the Buddha was present in their lives.

Or they may have moved to the city before their parents had a chance to impart enough knowledge about their ancestors, and so it seems natural to them to live in a home without an altar. Over the generations, our fine tradition is gradually being lost.

I can't help feeling that there is a connection between this and the sense of disenchantment that people feel today.

The act of putting your hands together before your ancestors is not merely a ceremonial ritual. It is a way of expressing gratitude for the life we have now, for everything that has been passed down from generation to generation. There is not a single person among us who would exist without our ancestors.

I start each morning by putting my hands together and saying, 'I am grateful to greet another day in good health.' And every night, with hands together again, I convey my appreciation: 'I am grateful for making it through another day.'

Sometimes, I have conversations with my ancestors.

Each of us has various experiences as we go about our days. There are mistakes that happen at work and complications in our relationships, things that tie us into knots and drag down our spirits.

You can talk to your ancestors candidly about all of these matters. It's surprising how authentically yourself you can be before your ancestors.

Of course, it's not as if your ancestors will offer a reply, but by unburdening your feelings, you will feel peaceful and calm. Doing so will relieve any sense of disenchantment and inspire a positive frame of mind.

You could also say that the time you spend with your ancestors offers your spirit a chance to settle. And not putting your hands together in gratitude – well, that's precisely one less opportunity to quieten your mind.

Of course, setting up an altar may not seem like the easiest thing to do. However, there's no need to be overly particular about it.

You can simply display photographs of your ancestors. Choose a spot in your home where you will be able to sit. Whenever your heart feels heavy, or a sense of disenchantment looms, go there and be still as you put your hands together, then stay a while as you unburden your thoughts. I'm certain that by doing so, your mind will feel more settled and your outlook will be more positive.

This spot that takes up only a tiny area of your living space will have a dramatic effect on your spirit. Whatever has burdened your mind or afflicted your heart will go away.

This is what it means to have a spiritual abode. I urge you to create one for yourself.

4. PARE DOWN YOUR BELONGINGS

It will lighten both your mind and body

Once we acquire things, it can be difficult to part with them. All of us can relate to this sentiment, to a greater or lesser extent. In fact, it may even become a source of distress.

I often hear people say, 'My home is too cramped. I don't know when I got so many things.'

Just after you move in, your home is neat and tidy and it seems like there is plenty of room to live comfortably, but before you know it, the place is filled with things and it's anything but a relaxing space . . .

This has a depressive effect. I'm not talking about hoarders who live in 'garbage mansions', but I think everyone has more than a little experience with this.

The cause is strikingly obvious.

It's due to an inability to part with things, an unwillingness to throw things away.

In Zen, we have a word for alms-giving: *kisha*. It means gladly giving something up, without regret. This is how we describe it when you toss coins when visiting a temple or shrine.

Why would anyone be glad to give up something as important as money?

The reason is that by getting rid of things, we give up some of our own attachments.

Since attachments are likely to cloud our minds, letting go of attachments has the power to make us feel happy.

This also applies to things.

Take a quick look at the things that surround you. Is there clothing stuffed in the closet or dresser that you haven't worn in years? Do you have bags that you used once or twice or various trinkets taking up precious space?

'I'll use this some day . . .'

This is always the excuse used to justify keeping something around. But if you haven't even thought about it in the last three years, do you really believe that the impetus to use it will come around soon? Will you ever again use a bag that hasn't seen the light of day in five years? The answer is most likely 'no'.

If this sounds familiar, you must let go of your feelings and dare to get rid of things. I recognize this may conflict with the mentality of not letting things go to waste.

It's true – it can seem wasteful to cast things aside. But it's a question of how you go about getting rid of them.

If a friend or someone you know might wear it or be able to use it, you can give it to them, or donate it to a charitable organization. Another place to dispose of it is a flea market.

Any of these options aligns with the mentality of not letting things go to waste while still holding true to the *kisha* spirit of alms-giving.

Disposing of things that you ought to get rid of will create more space, which will increase the comfort of your home and improve your daily life. Needless to say, this will have a positive effect on both your physical and mental wellbeing.

Some items ought to be kept – things that cannot be thrown away, regardless of whether you use them. These include keepsakes and mementos inherited from parents and grandparents, and items you bought specifically for the family or to commemorate something special.

The challenge lies in determining what falls into which category.

To my mind, the most important factor is how you feel about each thing.

When you hold it in your hand, does it stir up memories and warm your heart? Does it remind you of the person who gave it to you and make you happy? Does it make you feel relieved or invigorated?

This has nothing to do with monetary value. There are some things worth keeping, no matter how old and tattered they are, even if they're broken. These items are much more than simply 'things' – they are intimately connected with your life. Find a beautiful box where you can tuck these tokens away and save them.

In Zen, we speak of 'walking hand-in-hand'.

This means going through life with those in whom we truly believe and trust – including our essential selves. The things that enable us to safeguard our memories are in no small part responsible for this feeling as well.

5. JUST BE, AS YOU ARE

Don't focus on things you have no control over

– – – – –

Putting every ounce of your strength into whatever it is
you're doing . . .

This strikes me as an admirable way to move through life.

But as something to live by, it seems we should be sure to keep
the following in mind:

There are things in this world over which we have no control.

Do you have a tendency to think that you must give
everything your all, that one way or another you must boldly
try to make things as you want them to be?

And yet, there are things that we really don't have any control
over. We can dedicate all our energy to something, we can
tackle it with our whole soul, but nothing is going to change.
No matter how hard we try, we will only wear ourselves out
and suffer for it.

This one life that we are given is filled with things we have
no power over.

For instance, are you capable of stopping your heartbeat? Your heart functions of its own accord, and there's nothing you can do about it. Life itself consists of things we have no power over, things that are beyond our reach.

There is a reason why, in Buddhism, we believe we are guided by a force greater than ourselves – be it macrocosmic truth or Buddha nature – rather than by our own authority.

When we realize that the point from which our life force springs is beyond our control, it becomes easy to recognize how many other things fall into that category. Isn't it a relief to learn that there is no need to exhaust ourselves?

So, it's best to accept as they are these things we have no control over.

No matter how much care and attention we might devote to our health, we still suffer from sickness or injury.

We might complain, 'I was trying so hard to take care of my health but I still got sick . . . I must not have been paying enough attention!' But what we are doing is discrediting the reality that we are, in fact, sick. This simply doesn't make any sense. What's more, by condemning and blaming ourselves, we become progressively more negative in our thinking.

The Japanese characters for 'sick' illustrate that it is our spirit that is pained. Thus, when we are sick, our spirit falters, which then has an effect on our condition.

Often when we're injured, a part of the body is impaired.

'Oh, I can't move like I used to . . . Why did this have to happen to me?' Cursing your fate will not restore your physical capacity. It will only make your days gloomy.

Both of these are instances in which we have no power. There is no option other than acceptance. You may try to resist, but in the end, you can only accept.

That being the case, why not do so readily?

As you are, without alteration – this is your real self. It is all that any of us can ever be.

Once you accept for yourself the things you have no control over, you will be able to live with the circumstances. You will be able to face up to what it is that your real self – as you are, without alteration – is capable of. You will no longer be fixated on the things you're powerless over, and you'll be able to deal with the things that you can manage with a positive outlook.

I used the example of health, but of course, in every situation, there are all sorts of things over which you are powerless.

Rather than focusing on those things, focus instead on what you may be able to control.

6. TAKE OFF YOUR COLOURED GLASSES

This will eliminate 90 per cent of your worries
about personal relationships

– – – – –

Our personal relationships can be downright perplexing.

It's probably fair to say that much of the anxiety, worry and fear that weighs on us involves personal relationships. Work, community, school, friends, family, siblings, relatives – there are many layers to our relationships. And sometimes, these get complicated and lead to the anxiety, worry and fear that cloud our mind.

'My boss and I just don't seem to see eye to eye. No matter how hard I try, I can't seem to make things work out.'

'I'm trying to be understanding, but my friend just isn't reliable.'

'The lady next door always acts like she's avoiding me.'

It's human nature that once we become fixated on negative thoughts, it can be very difficult to dispel them. In fact, you might even say that, by and large, the tendency is for them to intensify.

The boss you don't see eye to eye with is impossible, you start to question the very character of the friend who's unreliable, the lady next door who avoids you has it in for you . . . When you repeat these kinds of things, you bring about ill change.

But if you trace things back to where they began, the origin is almost always something trivial. You had a minor clash of opinion with your boss in a meeting, your friend inadvertently forgot about plans he made with you, and there was one time when you didn't respond to the lady next door's greeting . . .

These are all trivial matters, and in each instance, only one facet of the other person was taken into account.

This is what I refer to as wearing 'coloured glasses' – by which I mean having preconceived notions. They might not seem significant, but they can cause problems if they are given a chance to take root in your mind.

For example, have you had this experience? You're about to meet a new work associate, and you get a piece of information about them from someone else.

'Oh, yeah, he has a reputation for being difficult. You're meeting with him tomorrow? Well, better watch out. But maybe it'll work out.'

This won't do. Your new work associate has just been pigeon-holed as 'difficult'. It's easy to imagine how the meeting will go. Even taking into consideration a certain guardedness or nervousness, no matter how accommodating he might actually be, it's almost impossible that you'll be able to recognize his true nature. Hindered by the bias of your preconceptions, you'll be circumspect in dealing with him, which may end up offending him.

In Zen we say, 'Don't wear coloured glasses.'

It is a strong admonishment against judging people based only on preconceived notions.

If you base your evaluation of someone on just one piece of information, or a negative idea or emotion you have from a single facet of what you've seen of him, you will inevitably misjudge him.

First, take off your coloured glasses.

Furthermore, etch the following Zen phrase into your mind:

'All sentient beings, without exception, have Buddha nature.'

It means that we all have the capacity for the inherent purity
and perfection of the mind that is Buddha nature.

'What I've seen myself amounts to only one aspect of him.
Next time I will try to seek out his 'Buddha nature'.

Zen teaches us to believe that we all have Buddha nature
(kindness and understanding, warmth and magnanimity . . .),
and that if we try to see it in everyone, we will find that it
reverberates in our own heart.

When we remove our coloured glasses and see with clear eyes, we won't miss those momentary glimpses of the Buddha nature in others.

Once you're able to see people's various facets, you may find that the boss whom you didn't see eye to eye with now favours you, even if she's still strict; that the unreliable friend is easygoing and lovable, if a bit scatterbrained; and that the lady next door who was avoiding you can be shy at times but is unpretentious and has a heart of gold.

I hope you'll recognize that what is behind these negative feelings or opinions is actually you, wearing your coloured glasses. Once you take them off, your perspective will be dramatically transformed.

The Buddha nature of others will steadily grow more apparent to you. Once it is revealed, the irritation and aggravation you once felt, as well as the anxiety, worry and fear rooted in your personal relationships, will disappear before you even realize it.

7. BE GRACIOUS

Be quick to defer, regardless of your status or position

The more we hold tight to things, the more our unnecessary fears increase.

For example, everyone has a particular status where they work or holds a certain position in society. It's important for each of us to live up to whatever that is, but we are also liable to cling to it. This can be problematic. For example, say someone at work has taken over as manager or vice president, and all they care about is protecting their position. They act like they've had their eye on this job for a long time, and now that they've got it, they'll never give it up, no matter what.

Needless to say, such behaviour can cause trouble for the organization. It has a detrimental effect on the training and development of this person's subordinates and can lead to less openness in the organization.

A boss who clings to or is overly attached to their status or position is disliked by those under them – even if they may be the only ones who don't realize it.

We don't have a zengo for this, but in the Book of Documents, one of the Five Classics of Confucianism, it says, 'Pride leads to failure, and humility is rewarded.'

In other words, an arrogant and self-important person incites loss, while a modest person reaps benefits.

And it is important, when the time comes, to recognize when to hand things over graciously, rather than cling to our status or position.

Of course, in many companies, a boss doesn't usually have the authority to decide that their immediate subordinate should take over their position when they retire.

But they can start doing things like handing over to those under them final negotiations with their roster of clients, entrusting to someone else their responsibilities as committee chairperson, allowing a rotation of subordinates to conduct the morning briefing . . . There are many possibilities.

Handing over your responsibilities does not mean that you will be overtaken by your subordinates.

And come on, you've accumulated years of experience in this position. What's more, your experience gives you an advantage – you can offer valuable guidance and an unparalleled perspective.

Once your subordinates are no longer answering to you or being delegated new projects by you, some of them may be at a loss, they may be anxious, or it may take them time to adapt. But during this period, what they will be most grateful for is guidance from a voice of experience. More than anything, that is what will help them develop competence and realize their potential.

The polar opposite of the boss whom everyone hates is the boss who is dependable and reassuring. And of course, it goes without saying that they invigorate the company as well.

The more you believe in the need to protect your status or position, the more you sow the seeds of unnecessary worry, and the harder it is for you to find peace of mind.

If you're able to delegate easily, without clinging to your position, those seeds of worry that nagged at you will fall away of their own accord, and you will find yourself with a broad perspective and a buoyant heart.

Here is the death poem of Hosokawa Gracia, who was killed by her family's samurai retainer rather than be taken hostage:

'In this world, knowing the right moment to fall is what allows flowers to become their utmost. It is the same for us.'

Isn't it truly refreshing to see someone who knows when to quit and hand things over?

8. RECOGNIZE LIMITATIONS

We can work only within our own abilities

— · — · — · — ·

What kind of connotation does the word 'limitation' have
for you?

Most likely it's a negative one.

But let's try to look at it in a positive way. For example, it's
crucial to know what your abilities are when it comes to
doing your job.

But a surprising number of people are unaware of this. When
a job offer comes in, they're willing to take it, regardless of
how suited they are to the position.

However, because people can work only within their abilities, if
the requirements of the job go beyond those, then people will
be unable to do what's asked of them, and they won't be able to
deliver results, both of which are a major hassle for others.

What often happens is that when faced with things we're
unable to do, we torment ourselves, becoming impatient,
irritated, disappointed, and even miserable. It puts a
tremendous spiritual burden on us.

The key to not falling into such a predicament is to know your limitations, and to recognize when they will be put to the test.

Do you understand what I mean? By knowing your limitations, I also mean the abilities you do possess – that is to say, having a good grasp of how far they will carry you.

Those who know their limitations are not lacking – they can be expected to do their job. This is a matter of reliability. Whether it's conscious or not, they rarely toot their own horn or bluster about themselves, and those around them are more apt to put their confidence in them.

They avoid coming up against their limits. As a result, they're spared unnecessary mental distress and loss of confidence, and can maintain a calm outlook.

When you think about it this way, knowing your limitations seems like an important way to find balance.

There is, however, something else I'd like you to consider.

And that is the way in which you face your limitations.

'Is it really best for me not to challenge myself beyond my abilities?'

That may be one way to see it, but there's a better way, which allows for more freedom. What I mean is, see your potential.

For instance, you understand your ability to be at, say, a level of 10, but what if you were to get a job offer that requires someone who is a 12?

Would you quickly decline the offer, assuming that the job will exceed your abilities?

Because at that point, there may very well be a gap between your abilities and the threshold for this job. And the job may be difficult to do, at your current level, but if you have the drive to challenge yourself and are willing to work hard, you just may be able to make up the difference. And I believe it's worth trying to reach that threshold.

If, on the other hand, the job requires a level of 15 or 18, then as a 10 you would be completely out of your depth – there's no way you'd be able to pull it off.

But if the range of the challenge is to stretch from a 10 to a 12, then there is plenty of value in trying to push beyond your limitations. At least that's how I feel, but what do you think?

Once you clear the next level, you build confidence. And, of course, your ability increases. Naturally, the threshold is now also that much higher. But you'll be able to face it next time and continue to challenge yourself.

It's important to know your limitations.

But it's just as vital to set your sights on that next threshold.

I sincerely hope you will take these words to heart.

part two

Concentrate only on things you
can achieve here and now

*By doing so, you'll stop thinking
about unnecessary things*

9. RECONSIDER THE OBVIOUS

You'll realize the happiness to be found in the present moment

'We are perhaps most likely to overlook our gratitude for the
obvious things in life.'

I often talk about this in my lectures, but the best example
of something we take for granted may be the existence
of our parents.

It's a given that parents will be there, that they will devote
themselves to their children, that they will protect them and
come to their aid both openly and secretly . . .

Often we appreciate just how fortunate we are to have those
'givens' only when our parents pass away.

'I feel particularly sad about my mother's passing when
I remember how she always used to send my favourite foods
from my hometown.'

'I had no idea how difficult it was to deal with all our relatives.
My father was the one who always handled everything with
them, and I never knew how much of a burden it must
have been.'

In tangible and intangible ways, we don't realize how much we rely on our parents. Everything they do for us – which we take for granted – attests to the magnitude of our parents' greatness, and we often don't even acknowledge them.

Ekiho Miyazaki, the abbot of a Soto Zen temple, said, 'There is an appropriate way to do things, at the appropriate time, and in the appropriate place.'

Even after he turned 100, Miyazaki Zenji maintained the same ascetic practices as those of young monks.

I know that his words seem obvious.

But I believe what he meant was for us to be all the more grateful to realize that this state of obviousness is, in itself, Zen enlightenment.

What if each of us took the time to reconsider the things around us that we take for granted? In the morning, we get up and breakfast has been prepared. We go to work and our desk is undisturbed. When something happens, good or bad, we say the word and our friends join us for a drink. We can tell just by looking at our children's sleeping faces that they are growing up just fine . . .

These 'obvious' things that are here right now, how much do they support and nurture us, or offer us comfort, encouragement and inspiration?

I ask you to take notice. By doing so, you will experience a major spiritual change. The irritation you felt towards your family, the job done carelessly, the friend who wasn't there for you . . . all that will disappear. You will be fulfilled by this moment, here and now.

Once you begin to cherish the things you've always taken for granted, you'll soon feel grateful for everything. Even boring, annoying and depressing things . . . With that attitude at the front of your mind, you can always maintain a sense of gratitude, and this will have a profound effect on your life.

10. DON'T RUSH, DON'T PANIC

Once a day, make sure to stand still

—·—·—·—·—

'All my life, I've just kept running towards my goals.'

When you hear successful people say things like this, it's easy to be impressed, and at the same time you might think to yourself, 'Hmm, well, my life seems to be at a standstill; I must just be giving in to laziness.'

There are certainly people who run all out, without stopping, and their lives appear full and dazzling for it.

However, not everyone is capable of that.

Take a staircase, for instance – there are people who climb several flights in one go, while others take frequent rests on the landing as they ascend. Once they have caught their breath, they are able to keep up their pace with renewed vigour. It may be that this approach, while different from doing it in one go, has its advantages.

There is something similar in Zen.

We say that for every seven times you run, you should sit once.

There's nothing wrong, per se, with racing through life, but in Zen thought, being still is not a bad thing. On the contrary, Zen teaches that it is extremely important.

Stillness allows us to reflect on ourselves, to examine how we've been doing. To those who might say, 'There's no need for reflection – I have no doubts about how I lead my life!' – well, that may or may not be the case.

Others might wonder, 'Once I stop moving, won't starting up again be difficult?' But there's nothing to fear – just try being still and see for yourself.

I believe it's particularly helpful to pause when you stumble or fail. There is always a cause for stumbles and failures, and it's important to identify what that cause is. Pause in order to understand – that is to say, it's an opportunity for reflection when we experience failure, to examine how or why we failed.

If you move on without investigating the cause, you leave behind your stumbles and failures. And some day this will have an effect. Far off in the future, you will be reminded of the things you left behind, and you will have to go back to retrieve them. In other words, you will continue to make the same mistakes.

Konosuke Matsushita, the founder of Panasonic, Japan's largest consumer electronics company, once said:

'People who are open-minded enough to honestly acknowledge the cause of their failure – to say, 'This was a good experience; I learned a valuable lesson' – are the ones who will advance and improve themselves.'

To turn stumbles and failures into positive experiences and learn lessons from them, it's necessary to bring to light their causes. There are things that ought to be done here and now. And in order to address them, it's important to pause. Even a titan of industry has the humility to acknowledge this.

Of course, it's worthwhile – not only when you stumble or fail – to pause and consider, at your own pace, 'Is this right?'

It's an idea – 'Practice the pause' – that comes from a classical Chinese text. The concept is that at least once each day, it's important to pause and reflect on ourselves.

While we watch as our friends and colleagues race ahead of us, it may be unnerving to stand still. But both Zen and the Chinese classics assure us that everything will be fine: we can pause without worry. I urge you to make time to think about all sorts of things, not just how to get where you want to go in life.

11. RESPOND POSITIVELY

It's okay to feel down, but get yourself up again soon

There is no such thing as a flat, monotonous life.
Every life has its peaks and valleys.

'When things don't go my way – at work, in personal
relationships, with my health – my mood darkens and
I feel down.'

That would be one of those valleys. But when we find
ourselves at a peak, we might overestimate our abilities
or look down on others out of arrogance.

In Buddhism, we call this excessive self-confidence *zojoman*.
We can forget our imperfect state, falling into a prideful
mindset, as if we have already achieved enlightenment. This
creates a vicious cycle.

Of course, as human beings, we are not capable of maintaining
an unfailingly calm and tranquil mind in the face of whatever
events may transpire or circumstances we may find ourselves in.

The unparalleled Great Yokozuna sumo wrestler, Sadaji
Futabayama, holds the all-time record of sixty-nine

consecutive wins. But in seeking victory in a seventieth bout, he lost, after which he is said to have sent a telegram to his teacher that read:

'The Fighting Rooster eludes me still.'

These words refer to a fable by the Chinese sage Zhuangzi. The story is about the training of a fighting cock, which was groomed to be impervious to the crowing of other roosters. Once the cock reached a level of heightened awareness, ready to attack when warranted but otherwise as immovable as a rooster carved out of wood, he would be unbeatable. Having been ruffled by his opponent in his seventieth bout, Futabayama expressed in his message to his teacher his self-reproach for not yet having reached that level.

Even with his enviable temperament, technique and physical condition, Futabayama still wavered, and achieving the state of the 'Fighting Rooster' proved to be extremely difficult.

When bad things happen, or when we find ourselves in a tough position, it's okay to feel down about it. But then turn your negative mindset into a positive one. That is the Zen way of thinking.

Here is an anecdote about a Zen monk:

On a journey that was part of his ascetic training, a monk spent a night in a dilapidated shack. The conditions were so bad that leaves fell through a hole in the ceiling, and in order to ward off the cold, the monk had to pull up the floorboards to burn for warmth. Suffice it to say, he found himself feeling despondent.

But when he happened to look up, he saw moonlight shining through the ragged cracks in the ceiling, and he felt enveloped by them.

The monk realized that this was, in fact, an extraordinary experience. The forlorn thoughts that had occupied his mind dissipated, and he was filled with bliss.

The fact that the shack barely kept out the cold hadn't changed. But instead of that making him feel despondent, he was able to shift his mindset to find joy in the moment.

When you can't understand why certain things happen to you, it's natural to lament and begrudge the situation.

But that need not be the case. My hope is that you can find a more positive way of responding, by saying to yourself: 'I can get through this, instead of just letting it upset me. I can hang in there!'

People also say, 'G-d never gives us more than we can handle.' When things seem bleak, and you feel like your spirit will be crushed or that you're stuck between a rock and a hard place, remember this, and you will be able to get through it.

This is the kind of thinking that can change your mindset.

This is the kind of thinking that can bring you back to the here and now.

How else to find a different direction?

They say we shed our skin in order to mature, but it seems to me that, in order to do so, we must go through various difficulties or adversities.

In other words, difficulties or adversities present opportunities to shed our skin and grow. You might even say that we ought to welcome these opportunities.

The Buddhist monk Ryokan, who lived much of his life as a hermit but who was beloved by children, once wrote this: 'It is good to suffer a misfortune when suffering a misfortune.'

The spirit certainly has the power to change.

If we keep this in mind, we can see our trials and tribulations as the opportunities they are.

12. CHERISH THE MORNING

The best way to create mental space

– – – – –

I would like to talk about making use of your time rather than being used up by it.

To be sound in mind and body – even better, to live vigorously – it's important not to upset the rhythm of your days. If the time when you get up in the morning and when you go to bed at night is constantly shifting from one day to the next, you cannot maintain optimal health, nor can you endure the mental exhaustion it causes.

What's more, human nature tends towards laziness – we can be as lazy as we set our mind to being. If we give in to laziness, there's no end to it and things only get worse. It's necessary to put a stop to it at some point.

What if you were to create your own rules in order to maintain your daily rhythm?

It's worth paying attention to your morning routine.

Cherish the morning.

I cannot emphasize this enough. And among the rules for cherishing the morning, the most important one to take to heart is, 'Rise early, at the same time every day.'

By rising early, you will create space in your morning.

Some people sleep as late as they can, then hastily make coffee, only to gulp it down and leave the mug in the sink before dashing off to the train station . . . Does this sound familiar?

When the day starts like this, it's easy to imagine what the rest of the day will be like. With no time to spare, we're mentally on the run, and there's little room to breathe. And so we're likely to forget things, and there's a good chance we'll make mistakes.

Consider the following Zen saying:

'You are used up by the hours in your day, while this old monk can use his hours to the fullest.'

It's from Zhaozhou, a Zen master who lived during the Tang Dynasty.

It stresses the importance of using your time well, but starting off your day like a harried, slapstick comedy is exactly the opposite way of going about it. That is the epitome of being used up by your time, of being at the whim of it.

Rise early, let some fresh air into your room, observe the ever-changing season outside your door or window as you take a deep breath. That's all it takes to get your blood pumping and to fill yourself with vigour. Notice the chirping of birds, or the breeze, or the tree leaves turning colour – your sensibilities will be stimulated and enhanced.

While you savour a cup of tea or coffee after breakfast, both mind and body take in the briskness of the morning, and you are inspired to make the most of the day.

Doesn't that sound like a luxurious morning?

This is what it means to use your time to the fullest.

Again, when the day starts like that, it's easy to imagine how the rest of it will go. Quality time flows from one moment to the next.

I'll say it again: the key to making the best use of all the hours in the day is found in the morning. I believe that this rule of cherishing the morning is especially relevant for those who are coming up on retirement and for those beyond it. Retirement is a crucial juncture in your life, a turning point in how you go about your days. All the more reason why not addressing it with care can lead to problems. If all you've ever done is throw yourself into your work, then when your work is gone, it's easy to lose your drive or for your spirit to flag.

In a pattern typical of this, someone reaches retirement and then seems to age all at once. A formerly dauntless corporate warrior becomes the pitiful guy who is now always in the way at home – this is not at all uncommon.

He gets up in the morning whenever he feels like it. He putters around until noon, decadently idle. Without anything to do, he leaves the television on a programme he has no interest in and just sits there, not really watching it . . .

If you allow yourself to become like this, then this could easily become the rhythm of your daily life. And from there, unnecessary anxiety, worry and fear begin to take hold.

It may be time to retire from your career, but nobody says you have to retire from life. We must treat with the utmost care this precious life we have been given.

And as I said, the morning is the key.

Just as when you were active in your career – even more so, actually – begin each day with the awareness of how much the morning matters. By doing so, your days will brim with vim and vigour.

It will renew your senses – perhaps you'll start looking for some other kind of work, or volunteer, or devote yourself to the hobbies you never had time for when you were working . . . I promise you, one of these will happen to you. Wouldn't it make for a lovely retirement to brush up on your cooking skills and treat your family to lunch every so often?

This one simple rule, to cherish the morning, will chase away feelings of hopelessness – that there's nothing to do today or any day – and will bring about an enriching period when you experience living in the here and now to the fullest.

13. LIVE BY YOUR OWN STANDARDS

Don't be swayed by other people's values

As we go through life, we're all acutely aware of
social etiquette.

Society is maintained on the basis of our shared version of
social etiquette. If each of us were to deviate from it and do
whatever we liked, society would devolve into chaos.

Social etiquette is worth upholding. But it seems to me that
it's possible to adhere to it at the expense of our sense of self.

When we are bound by social etiquette, we limit our
imagination, we're unable to act freely, our mind becomes
rigid. Don't you sometimes feel as though you're fettered,
hand and foot, by social etiquette?

In order to free ourselves, we need our own standards, so as
to avoid taking the wrong path in life. We must have a basic
foundation of social etiquette, supported by our own
interpretation of things and by guiding principles that enable
us, on occasion, to stray from the norm and make our own
decisions. I think of these as standards.

So, how do you develop these standards?

The only way to do so is to put them into practice yourself –
by accumulating experience.

Zen prizes practice above all else.

There is a zengo that teaches us, 'Spiritual enlightenment
comes only through personal experience.' Looking at water in
a vessel, you cannot tell whether it is cool or warm – the only
way to determine this is by tasting or touching it. It is more
important to act than to think.

Now that information is in abundance, knowledge – as much
as we want – is easy to come by. If you do an internet search
for 'How to live free of social etiquette,' you get thousands
of results.

But if you take the time to read them, you'll see they address
a range of unrelated subjects.

If and when you find yourself in a situation that calls on you
to decide whether you are bound by social etiquette, the sheer
amount of knowledge crammed into your brain is not what
will help you.

By accumulating experience and putting things into practice,
your body learns – that is to say, you are able to make the right

decision with guidance from your body – and of course, the proper action soon follows. You cannot develop standards from knowledge alone.

Koshu Itabashi, who was the abbot of a Soto Zen temple, would apply himself to the practice of sitting zazen or doing the temple chores of *samu* as if he were a monk in training, not the chief priest.

Seeing someone of his stature doing these things, the monks would say to him, 'Surely there's no need for you to do *samu*. Please, rest comfortably in your room.' But Itabashi Zenji would wrap a *tenugui* around his head, put on his work clothes, and do the cleaning with the rest of them. I heard that, even after he retired, he would sometimes still go out and beg for alms.

Of course, this exceeds what is required by social etiquette, but it demonstrates that a superb standard must have been established. Always in search of his own standards, however, Itabashi Zenji never strayed from his practice, continuing to accumulate experience.

Surely, this is the embodiment of inexhaustible Zen teaching. Standards are honed by practice and experience, and as they become perfected, the freer one becomes.

There is a passage in *The Analects* of Confucius:

'At seventy, my mind's desires do not exceed the standards.'

What Confucius means is that following his desires and taking action do not transgress what is right.

It's about living freely on your own terms (regardless of whether you adhere to social etiquette), and how doing so enables your innate truth to correspond with the way you live your life. This is what happens when you develop the standards that have been honed within your heart.

So please, I urge you to develop your own standards by keeping in mind: practice first and experience second.

Your standards will become refined, even if just a little at a time. You will find yourself more confident, you will be liberated from the anxiety, worry and fear that come from comparing yourself to others, and you will become free to be yourself.

14. DON'T SEEK OUT THE UNNECESSARY

Stop bingeing on information

I'd like to talk about the relationship between our information-driven society and our hearts and minds.

We are living in a highly networked age when information is abundant. And needless to say, the rapid evolution and spread of the internet has only spurred that further.

To be sure, there is something desirable about the convenience of being able to access a wide range of information, but at the same time, I feel that it may also be fraught with problems.

What I mean is, too much information inhibits our ability to make decisions.

For example, say you're thinking of doing something to improve your health. 'Maybe I'll look into this a bit,' you say to yourself and then do an internet search, only to be overwhelmed by a flood of information.

Looking at the search results, you find there are too many choices – and you lose confidence in making a decision.

'This seems good, but this seems effective too. Then there's this thing as well? And I can't rule out this one either . . .'

This happens in every kind of situation – at the workplace too. 'This seems promising.' 'Let's add that condition here.' 'If that's of interest, perhaps we should try this?' 'In terms of salary, this might also be good . . .' and so on.

When it comes to your career, the most important question to ask yourself is, 'What do I want to do?' Your choice of job profoundly affects how you'll live your life.

Figuring out what you want to do or how to live is not a matter of how much information you accumulate. The answer can be found only within yourself. And to find it, you must set about giving these questions thorough consideration.

To put it another way, it's a matter of questioning your heart, and deciding where to focus your efforts.

In this context, information can be a source of doubt. Counterintuitively, when you have an excess of information, your mind doesn't know what to do with it. And when your mind is untethered, doubt creeps in, along with anxiety.

At one time, almost everyone in Japan worked in the family business, from generation to generation. Farmers are the typical example of this, but also craftsmen and artisans handed down their skills from parent to child to grandchild and so on.

Without any choice involved, people's efforts were focused, and they were able to dedicate themselves to their work. And the fact that they were fully engaged contributed to their sense of fulfillment in life.

You might even say that not having a choice left no room for doubt or anxiety about their work. But neither were people tormented by idle illusions and anxieties the way people today are – and not just about work but also about life in general.

Of course, it's important to note that more choice means broader possibilities. But the key is to narrow the options. Think of it this way: put the emphasis on deciding where to focus your efforts, then gather only the information deemed necessary to that end – you will still find various options.

When you've questioned your heart and then chosen work or decided upon a course of action based upon what it told you, you will no longer waver – even if the results you hope for aren't immediately forthcoming.

Try your best to put this into practice. And here is the important point, as Rinzai Gigen, the founder of the Rinzai school of Buddhism, said:

'Be master wherever you go – then wherever you are, things are as they truly are.'

This means that no matter what the circumstances, if you try your best to do what you're capable of in the here and now, you will realize your potential protagonist, or who you're meant to be.

A protagonist is not misled by information run rampant, does not allow their focus to be drawn this way and that. Their gaze is fixed steadily in one direction.

A protagonist stands firmly on the ground, carving a path of their resoluteness. You could even say they are leading their life with certainty.

We are all capable of becoming our own protagonists, anytime and anywhere.

But first, we must focus our efforts. Concentrate on the here and now.

Why not begin there?

15. SHINE WHEREVER
YOU FIND YOURSELF

If not now, when?

— — — — —

Are you genuinely engaged with the work you do?
Do you take pleasure in it, and do you enjoy every day?

Now, I don't have data to back this up, but I have to imagine
that quite a number of people would be likely to respond to
these questions with 'Not really.'

It seems to me that many young people have a tendency to
give up quickly on their jobs or simply abandon their position,
saying that the work doesn't suit them, or that they feel like it
isn't what they're meant to be doing.

The Japanese version of the proverb 'Patience is a virtue'
makes reference to three years atop a rock, with the
implication that everyone has the wherewithal and resolve
to persevere in whatever it is they are applying themselves
to. This notion, however, seems like a relic of the past,
a sensibility that is now obsolete.

People nowadays seem to be disaffected, to lack a sense of
vigor. This appears to be a common sentiment. It may sound

hostile, but I can't help thinking that a dominant characteristic of this generation is a tendency to deem everything – from work to personal life – as 'boring'.

Boredom leads to discontent and grumbling, which become the seeds of worry. Ask yourself if the following hold true for you:

Are you able to genuinely engage with work, no matter what it is you're doing? However you are leading your life, are you able to excel at it and take pleasure in it?

What was your answer?

One thing is certain: genuinely engaging work does not simply materialize out of nowhere. You cannot just wait around for the life you want to arrive.

So, you must fully engage with the work you're doing here and now. There is no option other than to take pleasure in the moment you're living through.

There is a zengo that offers a hint about how to do this: 'Change the great earth into gold.'

It means that no matter where you find yourself, do your best and give your all, right here and now. This will make the place where you find yourself glimmer and shine like gold.

There's no such thing as brilliantly gold earth. It's you who make it so. Even if you feel like your job doesn't suit you, or it isn't what you want to be doing, make the work that you're engaged with here and now your own.

If you don't genuinely engage with what you're doing here and now, then where and when do you think you ever will?

There is a well-known episode from the life of Dogen Zenji.

Early in his training, he went to study under the teacher Rujing at Tiantong Mountain in China. One day, Dogen Zenji saw an old priest who served as the head cook in the temple, laying out shiitake mushrooms to dry in the summer heat, and not wearing a hat in the blazing sun. Dogen Zenji called out to the old cook: 'Why must you do this work now, when it's so hot? Perhaps wait until the sun's rays are not as strong . . .'

To this, the old priest replied, 'There is no time but now.'

What he meant was, 'Just when should I do it, if not now? When will the appropriate time be? That time will never come.'

Dogen Zenji is said to have been deeply impressed by the old cook's words. If you set your mind to accept that we have only now, that we have only here, you may learn a trick to spiritual improvement that will enable you to get serious about your work and about enjoying life.

You will see how to put your own spin on the work that you assume anyone can do, and come to appreciate that it's not just the same old thing.

You may even find that you're filled with an urge to do your best in the here and now. And then the world that surrounds you may appear completely different than it was before.

By putting your own spin on things, work that anyone can do becomes work that only you can do in your particular way.

Others may even start to wonder how they can do things in a manner that mirrors yours.

That is how you make an impression, and create a presence.

When you apply yourself wholeheartedly, then you are able to fulfill the moment and take pleasure in it. Doubt and anxiety vanish, and you see things more positively.

And then, in the here and now, you shine.

Plant your feet firmly on the ground wherever you find yourself, and you will flourish.

16. DON'T GO AGAINST YOUR FEELINGS

This is how to be unfettered by things

You're always fretting over things, or quick to get annoyed. How can you gain more control over your emotions?

To that end, I suggest the state of no-mindedness, what we call *mushin*.

When you are in a state of no-mindedness, you are not buffeted by your emotions. Rather than yo-yoing between joy and sorrow, hope and despair, your mood is always tranquil.

However, *mushin* is no simple task – it's quite difficult to achieve. Especially when sitting zazen – a kind of meditation – there can be a strong drive to 'empty your mind', and it becomes the very thing that fetters you. Your thoughts only end up circling around the imperative, 'Don't think of anything.'

When sitting zazen, the flood of thoughts popping into your mind is inevitable.

Let them drift up, and then let them float away.

They will dissipate on their own.

Give in to the flow of these thoughts appearing and disappearing. This is how you approach the mind-state of *mushin*.

When you toss a pebble into a pond, it creates ripples that spread outward. If you were to try to calm the ripples by putting your hand in the water, it would only generate more complicated ripples. By letting them be, you will see the ripples gradually settle down, and eventually the surface will be like a mirror again.

Your mind is no different.

There is a zengo, 'The cloud is egoless, it is not undone by the ravine.'

This means that the cloud is not fettered by anything, it changes shape with the wind, going where it is bidden, and yet never shifts from being a cloud. It manifests *mushin*.

We encounter all sorts of situations from day to day. Good things and bad things. Things that cheer us as well as things we can't abide. No matter what, though, if we allow ourselves to be fettered by them, we will be in great turmoil

'I can't believe he said that! What a jerk – I'm finished with him!'

We struggle to resist these bursts of anger that arise in our heart. We are consumed by them. As they fill our mind, turmoil sets in and refuses to yield.

Of course, human emotions are the essence of our being, so it's natural to give ourselves over to them, but as we try to do whatever we can to overcome them, they will always be foremost in our mind, and we will never get away from them.

A wooden stake that is driven into the earth becomes fixed and immobile. No matter how the wind gusts, it remains in place. Eventually, though, if the gale is strong enough, the stake is likely to snap.

Bamboo, on the other hand, is supple and bends in the wind, so even in a storm it does not break. Once the storm subsides, the bamboo returns to its natural form, standing tall and straight. It gives itself over to the wind – when it blows, and when it ceases.

There is no need to be indifferent to intense thoughts and feelings. Simply give in to the flow of them as they appear and disappear.

This is how to be unfettered by them. When you notice them, allow the tension to slacken and focus on 'now'. Your mind will relax and become supple.

And here we go, approaching *mushin*, the state of no-mindedness.

17. MAKE YOUR EVENINGS CALM

Late at night is not the time to make big decisions

⸺ ⸺ ⸺ ⸺ ⸺

Let me ask: are your evenings peaceful?

Part of Zen practice is a nighttime zazen.

At certain Soto Zen temples, this begins around 8 p.m. For the monks, it is a nighttime ritual to quieten the mind before bed.

Consider this: night after night, do you find yourself in a bar after work, complaining into your glass? Drinking your troubles away may be a temporary solution, but it can leave you feeling not so great the next day, right?

Making your evenings calm is surprisingly difficult. During the day, the work rush obscures your anxiety, worry and fear, but at night, these are thrown into high relief.

Once your mind gets caught up in them, it can be tough to shake them free. I happen to think this is strongly related to the darkness of nighttime, but it's a hallmark of the night for worry to breed more worry, and for doubts to further take hold.

After a sleepless night, haven't we all had the experience of things looking quite different in the morning light?

Your problems don't seem so terrible, and you wonder just why you were so distressed.

Late-night decisions are also prone to error. What's more, turning all your worries over in your mind stimulates your brain and can make it impossible to fall asleep.

For this reason, one of the tricks to making your evenings calm is to avoid, as much as possible, having to make decisions at that time.

This advice is based on the experience of a well-known economist. The nighttime used to be when he'd gather information from TV and the internet, but at some point he decided to stop – he unplugged from all news in the evenings. And in the mornings he felt more settled than ever before, and more clear-headed about making decisions.

When you take in information, you can't help processing it and mulling it over.

Block it out.

This seems to be one of the most important ways to make your evenings calm.

Another effective way to encourage serenity is to make time for whatever makes you feel good and helps you relax.

Of course this will vary from person to person. Some people may like to read a novel or peruse the pages of a comforting poetry collection. If you like listening to music, make the nighttime your time for doing so. If you'd like to take up crafting or another hobby, make the evening your time for it.

You might like to light incense or your favourite candle and take a long bath.

When you make time for pleasure, you will naturally feel calmer and more at ease. Making this an evening ritual before bed is no less Zen than a nighttime zazen. You end up improving the quality of your sleep, and you will awake refreshed and ready to face the day.

part three

Step away from competition
and things will fall into place

'Everyone is their own person,
and I am who I am'

18. DON'T FIXATE ON VICTORY OR DEFEAT

It doesn't matter whether you win or lose

- - - - -

'I can't let that guy who started when I did get promoted above me!'

'They posted the department's rankings for the month – what to do?'

Because performance-based systems hold such sway in the modern workplace, anyone in business is going to be keenly aware of their accomplishments.

Which leads to comparing your results to those of others.

It's as if you're in a competition.

Of course, competition can be motivating.

But at the same time, it reduces everyone to merely winners or losers – so that if you outperform the guy who started at the company at the same time as you, then you're on top of the world, but if your performance isn't so hot, then you fall into a total funk. You're always at the mercy of these emotional vicissitudes. That is, undoubtedly, one aspect of competition.

It seems to me that the source of a significant amount of work stress is this excessive emphasis on winning and losing.

What's more, if all you ever think about is winning and losing, it encourages a win-at-all-costs mentality. This can lead to you keeping to yourself information that was meant to be shared with your colleagues, and secretly hoping they will make mistakes.

This is regrettable. But it's not so unusual in the business world for people to trip others up or to stab them in the back.

This is when we start to run into problems.

Suppose you manage to win by doing whatever it takes. Would you not have any qualms about celebrating your victory? Would you not feel any guilt about the way in which you won?

Winning at any cost leaves behind bad feelings.

It's just human nature.

Isn't it time to let go of this fixation on winning and losing?

There is a zengo, 'Even when the eight winds blow, do not be moved.'

We are affected by various winds in our life. Sometimes favourable winds blow our way, and at other times adverse winds rage around us. But if we remain unmoved by each of these winds, then we can appreciate all of them.

When our performance surpasses that of our colleagues, it feels like a favourable wind. But when we've fallen behind our colleagues, we may experience this as an adverse wind. This, though, is not 'winning' and 'losing'.

It's simply the blowing of various intermittent winds. We should just see them as part of nature.

To do so is to face these situations with sincerity.

This means that rather than look at things from the perspective of someone else, we must look inward, at our own heart.

'Did you give this project everything you had?'

'You settled for leaving things at that stage, but don't you think there's a bit more you could do?'

Of course, there may be times when you can honestly say you gave something your all, that you put all your energy into it. When you can say with sincerity that you tried your hardest, then that's enough.

And at those times you will feel a sense of satisfaction with the work you've done.

That sense of satisfaction is what's most important. Or at least I think it is.

Because as long as you are satisfied, you will be able to accept the outcome with serenity, no matter what it is. You'll be able to maintain a state of contentment, no matter which winds blow.

So shift your perspective from outward to inward.

The traces of victory and defeat will soon fade away.

19. KEEP AT IT, SLOW AND STEADY

Do this before you envy others' talents

— — — — — —

'Here I am, slaving away to finish this one project, and he's churning out one new idea after another like it's nothing.'

'It's a constant struggle to meet my sales quota. How is it always so easy for her?'

I bet this sounds familiar to many of us. At some point we've all been dazzled by someone else's talents.

But envy doesn't do you any good. Rather than be envious, here's something you should definitely do.

Learn to persevere and to steadily do your job to the best of your ability. Cultivating this habit will enable you to surpass your talents. That's how I see it.

The essence of Buddhist practice is to keep doing things over and over. During training periods called *seichu*, monks subject themselves to rigorous practice, day in and day out. *Seichu* last for one hundred days. The monks repeat the same thing, every day – sitting zazen, chanting sutras, working chores – and all these become habits. One way to put it is that the body learns and remembers.

Even if a monk has an intuitive understanding of Buddhist scriptures, if he neglects to put forth the effort required, then he fails in his training – he is not on the path toward enlightenment.

Ichiro Suzuki, the record-setting Major League Baseball star, said the following:

'I don't agree that a "prodigy" is able to succeed without effort. I believe that a prodigy succeeds because of their efforts. Anyone who thinks that my ability to hit a baseball does not require effort is wrong.'

Even Ichiro, a professional athlete with an abundance of talent, says that you can't be a prodigy without putting forth effort.

You could be as gifted as Ichiro – even more so – but if you don't apply yourself, then your talents will never flourish. Effort counts for more than ability.

There is a similar story in Buddhism, an anecdote about Zen master Kyogen Chikan, who was active during the Tang dynasty. Erudite and lauded as wise even before he entered the priesthood, he was deeply troubled by his inability to answer a koan posed by his teacher.

In despair, and recognizing his own obsession with knowledge, he burned all of his books on Zen. He then dedicated himself to tending the grave of the Zen master Nanyo Echu, who had lived to be one hundred.

All he did, every day, was clean the master's grave. But one day, as he was sweeping, his broom sent a shard of tile flying, and the shard struck a bamboo tree, making a clinking sound. Upon hearing this clink, Kyogen Zenji was enlightened.

And there you have the importance of assiduous effort, of doing the same work slowly and steadily.

Talent may be innate. But it does no good to wish that you had another guy's gifts or that someone else would share her ability with you. Instead, it is up to each of us to determine how much effort we must put forth.

Pay no mind to the guy who racks up the sales. Instead, when you start work in the morning, do so each day slowly and steadily, with a pithy email to a client just to check in or to share some thoughts or information.

Do this for one hundred days, and you just might be the one who hears the clink and surpasses your quota with ease.

20. EXPERIENCE GRATITUDE

What you can accomplish all by yourself
doesn't amount to much

Okagesama is a legacy shared by the Japanese people. Literally,
the phrase '*okagesama de*' translates to 'the gods' shadow', but
it is most often used to express gratitude.

Japanese people have traditionally prized consideration and
thankfulness. For the farming that is the backbone of the
country, cooperative work is fundamental. Throughout
Japan's history, fields and rice paddies were maintained
through collective effort and watering – if you were short-
handed, the neighbours would help out. This was simply the
way things were always done.

Underlying it all was the notion of gratitude and appreciation.
But that sensibility has gradually been lost, and now it seems like
society is becoming more and more self-interested and selfish.

This may be most noticeable in the business world. It used
to be that people would approach their job in the spirit of
teamwork, with everyone demonstrating their ability within
their own position, but this approach seems to have been

completely subsumed by the widespread influence of a results-driven system.

'Improving my performance is my top priority.'

'If I could just get my numbers up.'

This sort of thinking accelerates the drive towards individualism and self-interest. The result is a work culture in which it's permissible to trip others up or stab rivals in the back as long as it yields personal success.

However, as I stated before, *okagesama*, or gratitude, is a legacy shared by the Japanese people.

In the tsunami that struck Japan on 11 March, 2011, towns and villages were devastated, more than ten thousand loved ones were lost, and livelihoods were destroyed. And yet many people still offered thanks to those who came to their rescue.

There is still good in this world.

The concept of mutualism – taking action for the benefit of both yourself and others, in order to coexist – corresponds with Zen thinking.

Okagesama originally referred to one's ancestors. It acknowledged that we owe our existence to those who are no longer with us, and that we remain under their protection. When we utter '*okagesama*', we are expressing our gratitude for this patronage.

You may feel as though you exist independently, but we all have parents. And each of our parents has two parents of their own.

Going back ten generations, you have 1,024 ancestors; twenty generations, and there are well over a million.

Take away just one of your ancestors, and you wouldn't be here now. You are alive today because they managed to survive. When you think of it this way, you can't help but feel that you're here not thanks to your own self, but thanks to your ancestors.

The same is true at work. No matter how capable you might think you are, there is a natural limit to what you can accomplish on your own.

A single-minded focus on your own success means you'll never be able to achieve in a bigger way. Eventually you'll encounter a job you can't handle on your own, and be made to realize the folly of your self-interest. When that happens, it'll be like slamming into a wall.

Learn to be grateful that whatever work you do is supported by others. Even a deal you closed yourself is not the fruit of only your labour. Weren't there people who helped you prepare the materials necessary for the negotiations? Maybe someone who is computer savvy helped you with the presentation? Or someone fielded phone calls and took messages from the client you were negotiating with? What about the person who served tea when your client was visiting the office?

It is thanks to all of these people that you were able to close the deal. When you are able to express gratitude towards others, the people around you will be glad to assist you in your endeavours. And whoever has that kind of support will be able to achieve even bigger goals.

21. USE THE RIGHT WORDS

Words possess awesome power

Bad news travels fast, the saying goes, but gossip and backbiting also circulate quickly.

There will always be a price to pay for gossip and backbiting.

To the extent that you talk behind others' backs or say bad things about people, at some point the same will be done to you.

Not only that, it's likely that the boss you've complained about will get wind of what you've said, making the relationship awkward and endangering your position.

In Zen we talk about 'kind speech'. We preach that one should treat others tenderly, and speak to them with affection.

'Kind speech arises from a loving mind, and the seed of a loving mind is compassion. We should learn that kind speech has the power to change the world.'

This is a quote from Dogen Zenji's masterwork, *Shobogenzo*. I hope you'll take this to heart – that by speaking to others with compassion, our kind speech has the potential to move heaven and earth.

To be sure, there's nothing wrong with making friendly jokes – in fact, these can serve to break the tension or lighten the mood.

Of course, nobody has one-hundred per cent good qualities all the time – everyone has the seed for spite. And no one is one-hundred per cent bad, either.

Shift your perspective and seek out others' good points – their redeeming qualities – and praise them. Most people, when praised, will not want to offend, and they will offer a compliment in return.

But it's important not to take the easy way and assume you can just flatter someone. This is rule number one.

Praise is pointless unless you really mean it. You must figure out what truly impresses you about someone. But most of the time we are not very good about giving compliments. As Goethe said: 'Why is there no end to such calumny? People seem to think that, were they to acknowledge the slightest accomplishment of others, it would diminish their own dignity.'

To feel that praising someone else takes something away from you is shameful, but no doubt there are a lot of people who feel this way.

A relationship in which genuine compliments are exchanged, in which two people recognize each other's strengths, can be spiritually enriching.

Let us cast aside these strange neuroses and prideful ways.

As the Chinese historian Sima Qian said, 'A wise man does not slander, even after a friendship has ended.'

How admirable. I aim for the same myself.

22. LET YOUNG PEOPLE TAKE CHARGE

Your turn will surely come around

— — — — —

Most people in business would say it's important to be on the front lines.

Of course, depending on the job, just where that is varies, as does the nature of the work, but in any case, the main idea is the same: to make sure your presence is strongly felt.

As we know from the speed of technological innovation, business tools will continue to evolve and there will always be a parade of new ones.

Depending on what kind of work you do, being proficient with technology is often a requirement for staying on the front lines.

This can prove difficult for people who are not digital natives.

In fact, when personal computers were first introduced, becoming adept at using them became such a source of stress that some middle-aged and older employees developed autonomic nervous disorders. This condition even got a name: it became known as techno-anxiety.

But flaunting your proficiency is not the way to maintain a strong presence. If there are star players below you who have certain skills, it helps to delegate appropriate tasks to them, and for tasks that require skills you don't possess, you can add to the team those who do have them.

By letting people take charge, you can train others and build purpose-driven teams. This seems to me to be one way of both doing your job and asserting a strong presence in the business world.

By daring to retreat from the front lines, you will be able to draw upon your experience and offer advice while monitoring the team's progress and redirecting its course when necessary – all of which would appear to be an excellent opportunity to demonstrate your presence.

In Zen we have the word *kankosui*, which means 'old awl'.

It refers to an awl whose tip has been worn down and that is no longer used. A brand-new awl with a sharp point can make a hole quickly and easily. But it can also cause injury.

An old awl with a worn-down tip isn't very practical if all you're thinking about is piercing holes. To be sure, though, it can't hurt anyone, and it does hold its own particular charm.

As people age, they too are no longer as sharp as they used to be. They may not be as quick to learn new skills. But they have a depth and variety of experience spanning many years.

How easily can people with less experience handle difficult negotiations? Are they able to manoeuvre around tricky situations? They're liable to trip up the uninitiated.

That's when the old awl comes in handy.

'Let me tell you how, in my experience . . .' you might say, having bided your time.

The old awl can model the refined skills that come with maturity.

23. ACCEPT YOUR CIRCUMSTANCES, WHATEVER THEY MAY BE

Regardless of whether they are favourable or adverse

'What? A transfer to a regional sales office? Why me?'

'How come these things only ever happen to me?'

Faced with an unexpected situation, anyone is likely to react like this.

Even when it's not a major change like a regional transfer – it might be someone who wants to be in sales but is stuck in general affairs or who wants to challenge themselves with strategic planning but ends up in accounting – examples like these breed resentment and grief.

The circumstances of our lives are constantly changing. And in difficult economic periods, our work circumstances in particular are likely to undergo big changes. But that is to be expected.

Everyone is familiar with the phrase 'All things must pass,' which in fact comes from Buddhism.

It means that each and every thing in this world is always changing, that nothing remains the same for even a moment.

We are in a state of perpetual transition.

This being said, the fact is that we readily accept good changes and struggle to accept bad ones.

But no matter how discouraged we feel or how much we fret, that won't change the circumstances. On the contrary, it serves only to increase one's negative feelings, creating a downward spiral of resentment and grief, and leading us towards a psychological dead end.

This is no way to think.

You are capable of taking advantage of whatever circumstance arises – the experience you gain from it can become a springboard for the future, towards progress; it can become what nourishes you . . .

Konosuke Matsushita, the founder of Panasonic, said, 'Regardless of whether your circumstances are favourable or adverse, the important thing is to move through them graciously.'

Truly a wise saying.

When you live graciously, there's no such thing as good or bad circumstances.

There is nothing else to do but to embrace where you find yourself.

If you end up in regional sales, think of it as an opportunity to build a network of relationships. You can focus in earnest on making connections, and pay conscientious attention to each client. This will quickly improve your outlook.

No matter the industry, having relationships based on trust with a wide range of people is a powerful tool and a valuable asset.

Similarly, by working hard in accounting and accumulating knowledge about bookkeeping, won't this serve you well in the future? Business plans supported by solid knowledge of accounting and by cost awareness are more likely to be feasible in the long run.

In Zen we say, 'Every day is a good day.'

This is not to say that life is a succession of good days. There will be sunny days and rainy days. Sometimes you'll be able to bathe in that gentle sunshine, and other times you'll need to bear up against the cold wind. But no matter what, you will gain the invaluable experience of having lived that day, and it becomes precious to your existence. The Zen interpretation of this is that all days are significant, and therefore there is always good to be found.

Your circumstances should have no influence on the way you live your life.

The way you live your life will affect how you perceive your circumstances.

24. DO TODAY'S THINGS TODAY

The secret to feeling unconstrained in life

'I'm busy.'

'There isn't enough time.'

'It's always a race against the clock.'

Plenty of business people feel this way.

In many societies, overwork is common, and it often feels like there is not enough time in the day.

Inevitably, work goes unfinished, and you can't help having a defiant or so-what attitude about it.

'There's nothing that absolutely must get done today, so I'll do the rest tomorrow, or who knows when . . .'

But this makes you feel only more constrained by time. If you postpone until tomorrow the things you ought to do today, then tomorrow starts off that much more compressed. When this kind of thing happens repeatedly, you end up being late or running out of time. Eventually you run out of mental space, and then you become impatient and irritated.

You may have heard the saying, 'Time and tide wait for no one.'

Time does not accommodate people's schedules – and the tide just rushes in, leaving us in its wake.

This is similar to the notion of impermanence in Buddhism.

Nothing in this world remains the same for even a moment; everything is always changing. Time has already moved on and will never return.

This may seem obvious, but its very obviousness puts it just beyond your awareness. I think it's important to keep it at the forefront of your mind.

Get done today what needs to be done today. There is no more effective trick for avoiding the race against the clock or feeling constrained by time.

Hakuin Ekaku is known as the restorer of the Rinzai school of Zen Buddhism, and Hakuin Zenji's master was Dokyo Etan, known also as the Old Man of Shoju Hermitage. Under Dokyo Etan's strict tutelage, Hakuin Zenji was able to achieve enlightenment. These were Dokyo Etan's words: 'Serious matters only matter today.'

Meaning that even the most important things are here only today – that is to say, dwell in each moment with a pure mind.

To dwell in each moment with a pure mind – this, I believe, means to do only the things that must be done.

Dokyo Etan also taught that no matter how painful are the things we have to do today, there is no other time to do them but now – that is how you overcome them. If we follow this logic, then when we put such things off until tomorrow, it only makes difficult things even more difficult.

Delaying whatever it is doesn't mean you can get away with not doing the work. You're still going to have to do it. And your time becomes only more constrained.

Don't judge what you have to do by how demanding or easy it is – complete the tasks in a methodical order. That's my own style.

I'm the head priest of a Buddhist temple, so I never know when I will be called upon for a funeral. Of course, funerals are the highest calling. No other work can be done during that time. It can be disruptive to leave things half-finished, because it's difficult to pick them back up when the flow has been interrupted.

That's why, when I'm working on a long-term project, I say to myself, 'I'll do this much today,' and then I make sure to complete whatever goal I've set for myself.

In addition to being head priest, I'm also a Zen garden designer, I write books, I teach at universities . . . so there are all sorts of things on my to-do list. People often say to me, 'Twenty-four hours isn't enough.' But I never feel that way – I don't feel pressed for time.

Do today's things today.

Now, why not complete the tasks that are before you right now?

25. DON'T SIMPLY RUN AWAY

Failure doesn't mean your life is over

Nobody wants to fail. But fear of failure at work can make you risk-averse. You tamp down your willingness to take on new challenges, and by prioritizing being 'safe', you can lose your drive and miss out on opportunities to grow.

Look before you leap, the saying goes. But if you look and then don't leap, or if you can't bring yourself to leap, you're holding yourself back. Failure is unavoidable. And if you try to hide your failure, you become secretive, which is even worse than failing: the attempt to conceal a minor failure can turn it into something bigger.

No matter the circumstances, the best response is to apologize – immediately and openly. Even if you manage to cover up your failure, that doesn't change the fact of it. Then when you try to get a fresh start, you have no choice but to take corrective measures.

I think it's necessary to readily admit your failure in order for everyone involved to feel like they have the full picture. That way, even if the failure has been concealed, then if or when it comes to light, no one need feel they are complicit.

Failure doesn't mean your life is over. There's no need to be defiant – what if you just resolved not to let the same thing happen again?

In Zen, we say 'All things come from nothingness.' It means that every one of us is born with nothing, and since that is our original state, there is no use forming attachments to things.

Not wanting to lose your job is an attachment. If you lose your job, you'll need to find a new way to support yourself, but there is no need to worry about this unless it comes to pass. Of course it's one thing if you damage the company's reputation or cost it a lot of money, but one or two mistakes is unlikely to lead to your dismissal.

Even if it does, that only leaves you back where you started, in your original state of nothingness. And everyone is blessed with the power to start over.

If you cast aside your attachment to the company or to your current position, you'll see there is no reason to fear failure. And you'll be able to be more proactive at work – you may even be better at expressing yourself and demonstrating your abilities.

Kazuo Inamori, who took over as CEO of Japan Airlines and led it through a restructuring after bankruptcy, is also a Zen priest. He once said: 'There is no such thing as failure. You cannot fail if you are challenging yourself. The only time you fail is when you give up.'

It's important to remember our original state, that 'all things come from nothingness.' I hope you'll continue to challenge yourself without fear of failure.

26. BE MORE TOLERANT

You be you, and let others be themselves

— · — — — ·

There is the saying, 'So many men, so many minds.' In a group of ten people, you will have ten different characters and opinions.

This extends to the office, where the people we work with – whether superiors or subordinates – all have different characters and opinions. Not to mention different outlooks on life.

It's natural to occasionally be frustrated with people whose life philosophy differs from our own.

Take, for instance, someone whose manager is very family-oriented. They might complain that he leaves the office at the end of the day because he prioritizes his family while everyone else is still hard at work. They may not see this behaviour as 'managerial'.

Another manager might criticize his subordinates for the socializing that he sees as frivolous, admonishing them about saving for the future.

Or a comma-counting boss will click his tongue and cast a derisive eye over his less than meticulous employees.

But I'll say it again – so many men, so many minds. It takes all kinds. Regardless of what other people's life philosophy is, finding fault with the way everyone else thinks is unreasonable. Of course, if it has a negative impact on the work, then it's necessary for you to call them out on it, but otherwise, the basic principle is to acknowledge various perspectives.

An inability to understand this seems to me to cause interpersonal strife at work.

Ask yourself: does the root of your frustration with your superiors or subordinates have anything to do with imposing your values on them?

Accept other people's way of seeing things. Doing so will eliminate dissatisfaction and enable you to be more carefree and light-hearted.

What's more, it will allow you to acknowledge each other's strengths and weaknesses.

Say you work in your company's planning division, and you're required to draw up strategy proposals and present them to your colleagues. The following situation might arise:

'I worked myself to the bone to get that proposal done, and this guy just comes in and makes his presentation based on my work and gets all the credit – it's a thankless job.'

But think about it: your forte is drafting proposals, so you ought to focus your energy on that and leave the presentations to your smooth-talking colleague. You get angry when you feel like someone else is taking credit for your work. So what if you said this? 'Leave the proposal to me. I'll do a bang-up job, and for your part, you can seal the deal with a great presentation.'

This separation of duties plays to each of your strengths while delegating away from your weaknesses, enabling each of you to enjoy your work more.

Over in your company's sales division, some people excel at the detailed calculations that go into deals, while others are very effective at client relations.

Recognizing each other's strengths and weaknesses allows for a harmonious division of labour, and everyone can be more efficient and productive. This ultimately benefits you.

One more thing I'd like to add: I have a strict rule of maintaining a tolerant attitude towards whomever I'm working with, for the sake of making things go smoothly.

The Confucian scholar and ancient Chinese herbal botanist Kaibara Ekken, who lived during the Edo period, said this:

'The sages, being sages, ought to be righteous with themselves and not with others. Ordinary people, being ordinary, ought to be forgiving of others and not of themselves.'

If you take this maxim to heart, then your relationships with those above and below you at work are nothing to worry about. You can carry on with ease and confidence.

27. GO WITH THE FLOW

Solitude is fine, but isolation is not

- - - - -

There is the saying, 'A man has many rivals,' which may be more familiar to people of a certain age. It may sound abstract to say that the world is such a harsh place, but there do seem to be people who go around making enemies.

Like the guy at work who aggressively pushes his own agenda. This takes a certain skill, of course, but it also ignores the friction that is engendered by it, and I can't help thinking that the discord he creates will someday present itself as an obstacle in his path.

Say you're working on a bigger project than you've ever taken on before, and you can barely manage to put a team together because you see rivals everywhere. You run the risk of hearing your colleagues say, 'You aren't going to be satisfied unless it's done the way you want it, so why not just do it yourself? We don't want to hear about total cooperation.'

But the company is likely set up as a collection of teams, and you may find yourself surrounded by can-do junior employees

who, at least on the surface, pledge cooperation, so it's easy to imagine making progress.

They say that leaders are solitary by nature, but they mustn't isolate themselves. When they do, they're unable to carry out their role, and then impatience and irritation take root in the ranks.

Any time you're in a position to lead and inspire, there is a flow that is beyond your control. Go with it. Water doesn't battle with the rock; it takes a slightly different course and keeps moving. It continues to flow, unerringly, towards its goal, finally emptying into the ocean.

'Going with the flow sounds good, but where does that leave me and my goals?'

Is that how you see things?

Going with the flow is not the same as letting yourself be carried along. Gauge the direction of the current, taking into consideration how fast it's going, and then, rather than pushing against it, go along with it in your own deeply felt way. That's what I like to think it means to go with the flow.

In Zen we talk about a flexible mind. We are taught to be pliant and accepting. Unwavering determination might appear strong and admirable on the outside, but it's also associated with mental instability and rigidity.

That tendency leads to a narrow perspective, to a slowing of action. And isn't that what causes stagnation? Even worse, the junior employees might turn their backs, leading the boss to stamp his foot in frustration.

Why not practise maintaining a flexible mindset, and be like water, going along with the flow?

28. DON'T JUST TALK FOR THE SAKE OF TALKING

Opt instead for a 'cordial silence'

— — — — —

In this section, I'd like to talk about the gift of silence.

I wonder whether you've heard someone described as being 'as eloquent as one is skilled'. It refers to a proficiency with speech as well as action, to someone who is tactful and doesn't make errors. Another way to describe them is worldly-wise.

The ability to communicate well verbally is important for building relationships as well as succeeding at work.

Being able to draw people in with a compelling speaking manner is a component of charisma. And at work, the way you speak can determine your success or failure.

So much so that not being an effective speaker can erode your self-confidence. The bookstore shelves are crowded with titles about public speaking in particular.

Zen teaches a different approach.

We have a phrase that explains how enlightenment is not dependent on words or writing, and how spiritual awakening can be attained only through intuitive discernment. That which is most important cannot be expressed in letters or on the page – the quintessence of Buddhist teaching is transmitted outside of scriptures or sermons.

You could even say this is a fundamental principle of Zen.

The Zen gardens that I design, especially those called dry landscape gardens, are comprised mainly of rocks and white sand. I must decide where to arrange the rocks, how many of them to use, what kind of wave patterns to rake in the gravel . . .

These are important decisions, of course, but equally important in the composition of a dry landscape garden is where to leave things out – that is to say, the empty space.

The profound stillness, the expansive calm you feel when standing before a Zen garden derives from the reverberations among the rocks, the sand and the empty space. The expressive power inherent in that empty space is what must be represented in the design.

In the traditional Japanese performing art of Noh drama, the silent pause takes on great significance. The audience perceives the significance, holding their breath during these tranquil moments.

Another example is the storytelling art of rakugo, in which the pause is heightened to increase the effect of the punchline.

Silence possesses tremendous expressive power.

At times it can even convey more feeling or deeper sentiments than words.

In professional situations, when expounding on the merits of your company's product, rather than speaking smoothly and fluently in a torrent of words, consider that it can be more beneficial to listen carefully to what your client's needs are, to what they are asking, in order to make a favourable impression.

Sales pitches tend not to factor this in. Inevitably, they come off as a 'hard sell'.

All the client hears is the usual recitation of benefits and advantages. They know you're not listening to them.

And once the client catches on to your hard sell, even the most gifted speaker will not be successful. Smooth talking only scratches the surface, in my opinion.

Listening, on the other hand, definitely has something to offer. What does it convey? Sincerity, for one. True salespeople, those who produce results, know that this is the better way.

Clients can sense that these people are listening attentively to them, factoring in their wants and needs. And once they do, often it fosters a sense of trust. They think, 'I believe what this person says' and 'If they say it, it must be true,' and they want to buy what you are selling. What's more, they want to buy things only from you.

This isn't limited to sales. Trust is of the utmost importance in any job.

Being a smooth talker will get you only so far, whereas a cordial silence builds trust. This being the case, there's no need to try so hard to be the most polished speaker, right?

There is a Zen story that demonstrates the gift of silence.

Vimalakirti was a Buddhist layman, and in a dialogue with a bodhisattva, he answered with silence. This is known as 'Vimalakirti's thunderous silence.'

Silence can have just as strong an impact as rolling thunder.

So for those of you who dread speaking, there's no need to worry!

29. ADJUST YOUR BREATHING

The Zen way of breathing that alleviates frustration and worry

– – – – –

There are times when we have plenty of energy to face challenges at work, but at other times we find ourselves depleted and lacking in motivation.

We are filled with joy when we succeed, and we grit our teeth when reprimanded by our boss or when something out of our control goes awry and makes us furious.

These mental shifts affect our behaviour as well. When our emotions are too intense, they can become a problem and can wind up giving those around us impressions like this:

'That guy gets carried away too easily. It's better not to encourage him.'

'You never know with her – she can be temperamental – so best not to take what she says seriously.'

The Zen expression, 'The ordinary mind is the way,' emphasizes the importance of cultivating a calm and quiet mind. It teaches us to decrease the intensity of our emotions.

The way to do this is through your breathing.

In Zen we speak of harmonizing our posture, breathing and mind. We adjust, in this order, our body, then our inhalations and exhalations, and finally our mental state.

This is the Holy Trinity – each of these is deeply connected with the others. So, in order to regulate our breathing, first we must regulate our body. We settle our posture, then we settle our breath, and then our mind will be settled.

When you feel the heat rising to your cheeks in anger, first, take a deep breath.

Focus your attention on your tanden – the point about seven or eight centimetres below your navel – and exhale fully, expelling all the air in your midsection. A full exhalation is important. In the Japanese word for breathing, *kokyu*, the character for 'breathing out' comes before the character for 'breathing in' – exhaling comes before inhaling. Once you have fully exhaled, inhalation follows naturally, automatically.

In order to facilitate the repetition of this kind of abdominal breathing – breathing from your tanden – you must lengthen your spine and straighten your posture. You cannot breathe from your belly when you're leaning forward or stooped over. When you practise breathing from your tanden, the anger that had crept into your shoulders will slacken, whatever mental strain you were experiencing will release, and suddenly you will feel more relaxed.

Now you may find that it is easier to deal with people. You may feel a bit more reserved, able to observe things with more detachment. Perhaps you'll see how foolish it is to get worked up about every little thing.

Earlier I referred to Itabashi Zenji, and I'll quote him again:

'Do not allow anger to reach your head.'

When we keep our anger to ourselves, tamped down in our belly, we can manage our intense emotions and avoid saying things we ought not to – and sooner or later, that anger will naturally dissipate.

Itabashi Zenji is also said to have recited to himself, 'Mr. Thank You, Mr. Thank You, Mr. Thank You' three times, as a sort of countermeasure against anger. Doesn't this seem like the perfect method for maintaining a calm mind?

It's a good idea for all of us to keep a mantra or an incantation on hand – whatever works best for you, whether a favourite word or phrase, or something that comforts or soothes you. Of course, you could recite the zengo, 'The ordinary mind is the way.'

It's not only for anger. You can use your breathing and a mantra for positive emotions, too, on happy occasions, or whenever your feelings are stirred up. It's important to modulate how you express joy too – being overly excited will only raise people's eyebrows. Come to think of it, here's another saying:

'In victory, remember your humility, and in defeat, remember your fighting spirit.'

Let's try to cultivate a calm and quiet mind.

30. CHANGE THE 'AIR' IN YOUR HOME

Do this first thing, as soon as you wake up in the morning

— — — — —

I believe there are several conditions for fostering a sense of peace and calm in your life. One of them is 'a room of one's own.' Do you have a space you can call your own?

For those of us who work, it may be our workplace – where we spend at least eight hours a day – that feels like our space. But there's a bit more nuance to the idea of a room of one's own.

Most workplaces are frenetic, enervating, emotionally charged, and nerve-wracking – hardly the kind of space where you would feel at ease. No surprise, since business is all about competing with people both inside and outside the company.

What's more, given corporate downsizing, layoffs and remote-work arrangements, you never know when you might lose that space.

For those of us who spend a lot of time at home when not at work, well, home might not be a peaceful place either. Spending quality time with your family is often difficult, and many families hardly even make conversation with each other,

with everyone fending for themselves for meals and doing
their own thing.

For some people, the bar or restaurant they stop in at for
a drink or a bite to eat on their way home from work
is their space.

I can understand that. But even if they derive a certain pleasure from that, it's a bit sad.

In Zen we have a saying, 'Return home and sit at ease.'

Simply put, it means that when you go home and make yourself comfortable the calm realm you inhabit will help to put your mind at ease.

In terms of Zen, home refers to the Buddha nature that resides in all of us – it's where we can be our true selves. Put another way, home represents the joy of discovering our Buddha nature.

That's really what home should be – the place where you are most suited to be.

Maybe you need a home reset to bring it in line with this?

You might think of it as a kind of renovation, but since one of the fundamentals of Zen is practice, it's really more about changing your relationship to the space.

Greet your family brightly when you wake up in the morning, and express gratitude for them.

At first, they might seem puzzled and wonder what's come over you. But after a week or ten days, they'll soften, and even come to appreciate the new space you're creating.

There is an anecdote about Hyakujo Ekai, who knew about the origins of the rules that govern Zen monasteries, which are called Hyakujo Shingi.

A monk once asked Hyakujo Zenji, 'What is the most wonderful thing?'

Hyakujo Zenji responded, 'I sit alone on this great sublime peak.'

What he meant was that sitting zazen was the thing he was most grateful for.

That great sublime peak was the place where Hyakujo Zenji was the chief priest – that is to say, it was a Zen temple. For Zen monks, the temple is their home. It brings them great security, and there is nothing for which they are more grateful. You might even say this is because they are enlightened.

So, home is a place of great security. Only more so as each decade passes. Think about when you wind down your career. You'll spend the majority of each day at home.

If that home is a peaceful place, if the atmosphere is refreshing, then your life will take on those qualities.

So please, start laying the foundation for your here and now.

I'll say it again: what is fundamental to Zen is practice.

part four

Surprising tips for
improving relationships

*How to form good connections
and let go of bad ones*

31. CHERISH YOUR CONNECTIONS

It's no accident that you happened to meet these people

– – – – –

How many people do you think you will meet
over the course of your life?

They will come in all shapes and sizes. And they will vary by
context – be it familial, educational, regional, work-related,
and so on.

Nevertheless, the number of people we will meet is extremely
limited, in a world with a population of more than seven
billion. But still, it's all but miraculous, those among the seven
billion whom we do come to meet.

Have you had an encounter that you consider to be a miracle?

You may think it's chance or coincidence that determines
whom you meet. But when you meet someone, there is a
connection at play. In Buddhism, we refer to these connections
as innen, and they are considered extremely important.
Among the multitudes of people who come and go over the
course of your life, those with whom you form connections
are special. This is because of innen – when the cause karma
and the condition karma are aligned.

With the arrival of spring, flowers bloom. But not all flowers will bloom at the same time, even on the same tree. Only the buds that have swelled up will catch the warm spring breeze and thus come into bloom.

Even though the spring wind blows the same way on all the buds, those buds that are still tightly bound up will not catch the wind and come into bloom. All they can do is sit on the branch as the breeze wafts over them.

In order to produce the effect (in this case, the flowering), the cause (that is to say, the swelling of the buds) needs to have had the right conditions in place to take advantage of the spring wind and to form a connection.

Everything in the world occurs according to this karmic connection of innen – this is a fundamental underpinning of Buddhism.

If we perceive our encounters with others in this way, then maybe there aren't any coincidences and nothing is by chance, and these miracles are a gift of the Buddha himself?

If this is the case, then we cannot make light of our encounters. We must accept our connections to people with gratitude.

In Zen we speak of the influence of those who come into our lives.

Everything is generated by these encounters. And so we must cherish the people we meet, the places we meet them, and the forms that these meetings take.

In the tea ceremony, which is deeply connected with Zen, there is the saying, 'Ichi-go ichi-e'.

This is a well-known phrase, even outside of Japan. One way of translating it is 'once in a lifetime'. It means you should treasure each and every encounter, because you may never meet that person again – this may be the one and only chance you have to be with them – so make the most of that time together.

If you adopt this attitude, then I think you will begin to cherish every meeting and to be filled with gratitude for everyone you encounter.

'How truly wonderful to have met this person.'

'How truly grateful I am to have crossed paths with them.'

This will enable you to forge much deeper bonds with the people who come into your life.

32. MAKE GOOD CONNECTIONS

How to create an upward spiral of good people in your life

– – – – –

Do you make good connections?

Or do you end up making bad ones?

All of us are born in possession of pure beauty, with a heart that shines like a mirror. As I've said before, Buddhism teaches that 'All sentient beings, without exception, have Buddha nature.' A newborn baby has no self-interest, no attachments, no illusions.

But then we're exposed to various people and circumstances, and as we accumulate experiences, our mind becomes clouded. How we form relationships with people has a tremendous effect on us.

People are bound together by their connections.

Once you make a good connection, it will be linked to your next good connection, which will attract additional good connections.

For example, when you establish a relationship with someone, you might meet someone else really wonderful through that

person, and then they may introduce you to another person with whom you make a good connection.

It can become a positively reinforcing cycle, and it's beneficial to you, with these personal relationships serving to enhance your network of good contacts.

On the other hand, if you make a bad connection, the complete opposite can happen. You can form a cycle of bad relationships – and before you know it, your life has become a mess.

In order to make good connections, preparation is necessary.

But what kind of preparation?

One thing you can do is to be as engaged as you can be, no matter what it is you're doing. You may think this sounds simplistic, but you'd be surprised by the extraordinary effort it takes to stay engaged.

By nature, human beings seek the path of least resistance. Once you start to slack off a bit, you're on a slippery slope, and you can find yourself cutting corners in everything you do.

Soon enough, people will start saying, 'That guy – whatever you ask him to do, he makes a mess of it.'

And once you're seen as a mess, no one is going to want to open up their personal network to you. No matter how hard you seek out good connections, they will remain elusive, and you won't be able to avoid making bad connections either.

Being surrounded with bad connections, you will feel your spirit cloud over, you'll lose stability, you'll be blanketed with anxiety, worry and fear.

There is a zengo, 'Every step is a place to learn.'

This is a favourite of mine – the idea that no matter where we go, there is something to learn, and that whatever we're doing can be a practice.

Zen teaches that everything requires discipline, and so we must devote the same kind of attention to practising zazen, eating meals, cleaning, even washing our face.

Applying this to your work, it would be unacceptable to give your all only on big projects, and then to dial it in on minor ones. This is what brings about bad relationships.

You must try your best on the work that you have before you. Doing so will naturally bring about good connections. Other people will take notice of you if you're working conscientiously on a project that might be undervalued or neglected.

Before long, your superior may ask you to join her team on an upcoming project. This will deepen your relationship with her, and begin a cycle of good connections.

33. YIELD TO OTHERS

One of the best relationship secrets is 'After you'

My work as a garden designer often takes me to other countries, and something I always notice is that every country really does have its own national character.

For instance, in some places, it seems like almost nobody ever yields to other cars on the road. And when someone wants to get into a lane, they just move ahead, and eventually force their way in. The roads have the feel of a battlefield.

It gives the impression that everyone is always trying to assert themselves, and in some countries this may very well be what it takes – you might say that national character suits the demands of the culture.

In Japan, by contrast, if you were to constantly put yourself first, your work and relationships would suffer.

Assertiveness is one thing, but self-righteous aggression makes it difficult to win support from those around you.

'That guy, he's never satisfied unless he's in charge, so let him do it himself.'

This can lead to people turning their back on you when you need cooperation and collaboration.

I think the best position to be in is second place, where you have the ability to say, 'After you.' The person who goes first is then out of the way, for the time being, and you are free to concentrate on bettering yourself or, in a work setting, on acquiring knowledge or skills or simple know-how.

In the strong second position, you have also been pushed to the fore, without even moving. This is the best place to be. In contrast to those who put themselves first, here you're less likely to be thwarted once you find yourself at the front.

Instead, you'll see that others are happy to lend you a hand. Before you know it, you've attained leadership skills even though you're still in the 'After you' second place.

In situations outside of work, the 'After you' mentality brightens things around you and makes others happy. When someone on the train tries to claim a seat at the same time as you and neither of you yields, the atmosphere becomes tense and uneasy. But if you say, 'Go ahead,' you get a thank-you and a grateful smile.

Or when out for drinks or dinner with friends, instead of scrambling to serve yourself first, by offering 'After you,' you will develop a reputation for being kind and gracious.

Most people are happy to be presented with the opportunity to go first, and it reflects well on you not to be jockeying for position. You assume a sense of ease and confidence; what could be more attractive than that?

There is a Zen phrase, 'Gentle face, loving words.'

I've already discussed kind speech, in Part Three; gentle face is different. The phrase comes from the Buddhist scripture 'The Longer Sutra of Immeasurable Life.' It teaches us to interact with others with a calm smile and considerate remarks.

A calm smile and considerate remarks are both included in the Seven Gifts of Spiritual Dana. When we put 'Gentle face, loving words' into practice with the former (a calm smile) as well as the latter (considerate remarks), we are offering two of the seven spiritual dana at once.

Yielding to others with the phrase 'After you' exemplifies the practice of 'Gentle face, loving words.' By putting 'Gentle face, loving words' into practice every day, we brighten our surroundings, spread happiness, and increase our sense of ease. It's almost too good to believe.

Life is an accumulation of days. Finding greater ease in each day goes a long way towards creating a fulfilling life.

I urge you to add 'After you' to your guiding principles.

34. DON'T WIELD 'LOGIC'

It's important for everyone to save face

— - - - —

I hear many people say that they mess up their relationships in unexpected ways.

What do they mean by this?

But first let's consider the idea of a 'win-win' – a situation that is advantageous to everyone. I'm not sure exactly when this phrase came into use, but it seems to have evolved from the thinking of Stephen R. Covey, the world-famous author of *The 7 Habits of Highly Effective People*.

It's related to what may be a very Japanese concept, the idea of 'saving face'. We'd do well to keep it in mind – in both business and personal relationships.

If you have a tendency to insist that you're right and to refuse to listen to others, it won't be long before your relationships sour and everything starts to fall apart.

'You don't understand – you're wrong. This is how it is!'

By believing, in this way, that logic is undeniably on your

side, or imposing your opinion on others, you're never going to make friends.

When you justify an argument by saying it's the 'logical' position, you are automatically putting yourself on a higher plane than the person to whom you're speaking. This does not foster a relationship of trust and understanding.

Surprisingly, though, there are many people who do this.

For those who read this and think, 'Now that you mention it, maybe I do always insist I'm right or on having things my way,' you ought to reflect on this. You may be messing up your relationships in ways you don't realize, and running the risk of behaviour that you may deeply regret.

You can find people everywhere who have confidence in what they're saying and think they're right. But even if someone's opinions or ideas differ from yours, it's immature to shut them down.

Only by accepting that others' opinions or ways of thinking are legitimate, even if we don't agree with them, can we make someone feel our generosity of spirit. And doing so will strengthen your position. It enables everyone to save face, and to avoid unnecessary friction.

There is no such thing as an infallible idea or opinion. There are many ways of seeing things.

I can think of any number of instances when accepting the ideas and opinions of others revealed the shortcomings of my own thinking and helped me recognize my own errors.

Enabling someone else to save face doesn't mean you have to surrender or bend your own position.

On the contrary, the wisdom of everyone saving face is that it allows you to expand and deepen your own thinking, as well as to facilitate relationships, produce results at work, and foster personal development.

By enabling someone else to save face, you create the opportunity for them to consider your opinion in good faith as well, which engenders a willingness to discuss their true feelings. Each side has something to learn from the other, generating a positive environment and strengthening the relationship.

The only thing you get from arguing someone into silence is an empty sense of triumph.

Would you prefer that to a relationship based upon friendly competition in which everyone saves face? I think you already know the answer.

35. SPEND TEN MINUTES
A DAY IN NATURE

Find the moment when your spirit will suddenly be liberated

– – – – –

'There are so many things to do . . . The day goes by before
I know it.'

People live their lives at such a fast pace, and everything is
supercharged. Our brains are on alert practically every waking
moment. It seems to me that our intuition and sensibility
receive significantly less stimulation.

Intuition and sensibility, rather than knowledge and
education, are the vital ties that bind people to each other.
Perhaps because our lives unfold at such a fast pace, people's
intuition and sensibility have grown dull, leading to awkward
or weakened relationships.

I believe it's necessary to allow the thinking part of our
brain to rest when we put our intuition and sensibility to
work. I'm not a neuroscientist, but apparently once we
stop thinking, the neurotransmitter serotonin is released
into the brain. This relaxes us and deepens our intuition
and sensibility.

This is exactly what you experience when you sit zazen. But I realize it may be difficult to practise zazen once a day.

And so I would like to recommend that you make time to experience nature.

'That's all well and good, but I live in the city, where it's not so easy to enjoy nature . . .'

Fair enough. Cities are not places where you can step outside your door and immediately be in nature. But you can still manage to experience nature on a small scale.

In the morning, open a window, or, if your apartment has a balcony, why not step outside and listen to the sound of the wind or to the birds chirping? You could go to a nearby park to see which trees and flowers are in bloom. Or gaze out of your window at night to observe the changing season and the phases of the moon.

It doesn't need to be for very long. For however much time you have, let your mind go blank as you experience nature. Use this time to allow your intuition to deepen and to regain your sensibility.

There is a zengo, 'When you see a flower, savour the flower, and when you see the moon, savour the moon.'

The meaning is that each encounter with nature should be experienced fully.

In other words, don't worry about unnecessary things; just let your mind drift, and give your body and soul over to nature.

If you feel like your mornings are too busy, or there isn't a park nearby, or you don't have time at night to look at the moon . . . how about taking a ten- or fifteen-minute break at work to go up to the roof and look out at the evening sun, or gaze down at the greenery in the park below?

'The sun has been setting a little earlier each day.'

'Ah, the leaves on the gingko trees are starting to turn colour.'

These thoughts will suddenly occur to you because you are in tune with nature. And as you gradually begin to deepen your intuition and sensibility, your mind will be freed from the vexations and headaches of your everyday interactions.

Now, let's stop using our brains and hone our intuition and sensibility.

36. MAKE PEOPLE WANT
TO SEE YOU AGAIN

The Zen way of cultivating charisma

– – – – –

There is an important principle of social relations: the key is
the Chinese character '恕' (jo).

Many of us feel that our relationships are strained or that
we're no good at interacting with people.

But social interaction is an important part of so much
of our lives.

For instance, in a work situation, if you say to yourself, 'Ah,
it's so tiresome having to meet with that client,' there's no way
the relationship will be productive. Or if the mere thought
of attending your neighborhood association's gathering makes
you feel depressed because you find it difficult to connect with
others, you won't be able to enjoy living in your community.

These are the disadvantages to having an aversion to
socializing. And an awareness of this aversion can create
more psychological stress.

'But there isn't much that can be done about this, is there?'

Is that what you think?

In my opinion, the way out is not all that difficult.

What's important is the Chinese character I mentioned before, 恕 (jo).

It appears in *The Analects* of Confucius, in a dialogue between Confucius and one of his disciples, Zigong. The disciple asked the master what is the most important practice to uphold for one's entire life. Confucius responded:

'What about jo?'

The definition of jo has been much debated. Some say it means 'reciprocity' or 'empathy', or perhaps even 'forgiveness'. Confucius gave a further response to his disciple's question:

'Don't do to others what you wouldn't like done to you.'

A familiar saying. This is the spirit of 恕 (jo).

It is a principle of social relations, and it is the essence of reciprocity. Whatever it is that you don't like done to you, don't do that to others. If you follow only this simple rule, you will be sure to see your social skills improve.

'It makes me angry when someone shows up late.'

'That guy's arrogance is so obnoxious.'

'She's quick to raise her voice, so I can't really say what I want to say to her.'

I expect that you have a number of things you tend to dislike in others. When you resolve not to do those things yourself, you'll see many positive changes.

If you're always on time for meetings, others will find you reliable; if you make an effort to be polite and courteous, others will feel that you matter to them. A calm manner of speaking fosters a sense of connection with others.

Reliability, a sense of mattering to others, happiness and satisfaction, connection . . . all will have a positive effect on your relations with others. And your social aversion will soon be overcome.

By taking yet another step, you can be proactive in doing for others what makes you happy when people do them for you, things that delight you and make you feel thankful.

For example, perhaps one time you stopped by a client's office, and you warmly recall how kindly they thanked you; or you're grateful to someone who always responds promptly whenever you send them an email; or you can't help noticing that a colleague brings coffee for everyone . . . you could try to extend to others some of these kindnesses that have been extended to you.

We can do well to heed the words of Confucius:

'Don't do to others what you wouldn't like done to you.'

By putting this into practice, you will find that you have started to develop charisma. And that people will want to get to know you.

Dogen Zenji taught a similar concept, which he referred to as doji.

He said that we should accommodate ourselves to the state of others – when they are joyous or when they are sorrowful, we too should feel these things – much in the spirit of the Confucian concept of reciprocity.

Now, do you still feel that same aversion to socializing?

37. ADMIT ERRORS RIGHT AWAY

Not only in words, but make the effort to convey this emotionally as well

⸻

What kind of history do you have with your friends?

Over the course of a long friendship, there are bound to be misunderstandings or things that are taken the wrong way. And these can lead to quite a few rifts.

I'd be surprised if there are any best friends who have never had a fight. What's important is how you deal with it, how you reconcile. If you're careless, then you can break the bond you've worked hard to create.

It would be a shame to let a misunderstanding or a clumsy apology ruin a true connection. It's not an exaggeration to say that your life would be less vibrant without it.

'Do not delay in making amends for your wrongs.'

This is a famous proverb from *The Analects* of Confucius, but putting it into practice can be difficult. Even when you realize that it was something you did that caused a problem, for some reason you hesitate to apologize. Is it really that difficult to express regret to such a good friend?

To which *The Analects* also says this:

'To err and not change one's ways, this is what it is to err.'

To make a mistake and not apologize – that itself is a mistake. While you're grappling with whether or how to apologize, the situation becomes only more complicated, and you risk not being able to repair the relationship.

An apology should always be immediate and personal. The longer you wait to do anything, the more difficult it becomes. Apologizing is no different.

Even if you say you're sorry right away but without any attempt at reconciliation, as time goes by, it becomes only more difficult. It's not hard to imagine how the other person would feel.

'When he says sorry right away, it seems like he doesn't really mean it . . .' becomes 'What's the matter with this guy? I wonder if he even realizes he hurt me . . .' and then 'Maybe that's the kind of person he is. I never would have thought . . .' and finally 'What a jerk! I can't believe I was friends with him for this long!'

It's just as important that the apology be done personally.

In Zen, we have the word menju, meaning face-to-face.

It refers to a master and disciple meeting face to face for the vital teachings of Buddhism to be conveyed, not in scripture or writings, but directly and in each other's presence.

This applies perfectly to apologizing.

While email has become our main form of communication, it's not adequate for conveying to someone how you really feel or what you truly think.

Think about if you wanted someone to apologize to you. If you got an email saying, 'Sorry about the other day,' would you feel like you had received a sincere apology? Or would you be offended that they did it over email?

This is not limited to apologies – any true feelings can be expressed sincerely only in person. Regrets, impressions, consideration for others – it's important to convey these directly and in person. The true depth of your feeling comes across physically – in your facial expression, the tone of your voice, and your deportment.

And this can be seen only face to face.

38. DON'T HESITATE TO ASK FOR HELP

Someone will be there to lend a hand

There is a zengo, 'Open the gate and you will find long life and happiness.'

Meaning that being open and honest will bring about many good things.

When you've been going through a hard time, when you've faced difficulties, when there's been too much for you to handle on your own . . . know that you don't need to take on all of it by yourself.

Open your mind. When you need support, instead of carrying the burden on your own, it's better to ask for help.

Modesty and perseverance are qualities to be proud of, but there are times when they can also cause hardship.

A typical example is caregiving. In societies with aging populations, the number of elderly people who need care will only continue to increase, putting a great burden on families.

'It's my father, or mother – or husband, or wife – so I have to be the one to care for them . . .' people think, so no matter how onerous, no matter how hard it is, no matter how much trouble, they keep doing it without complaint. And what we soon have are senior citizens as caregivers, the aging caring for the aged, which leads to an untenable situation and often ends badly.

Workplace difficulties, too, can become unbearable. There's the phenomenon of *karoshi*, or death from overwork. There's also depression caused by friction with colleagues or harassment by a supervisor. People can suffer beyond the limits of their endurance.

Please, do not carry the burden upon yourself. Don't hesitate to ask for help. Simply by expressing your feelings, you will put your mind at ease, and someone will be there to lend a hand.

'Suffering, if it is accepted together, borne together, is joy.'

These are the words of Nobel Peace Prize winner Mother Teresa. If we ourselves are open and honest from the start, and put our pain into words, it will reach the ears of someone who can help alleviate our hardships. Sharing our troubles will transform them into happiness.

There's no need to hesitate.

What is it that you want to talk about with someone now?

39. BE A GOOD LISTENER

Relationships are about give-and-take

— · — · — · —

'All that guy ever does is whine and complain. I can barely stand being around him.'

'I've had enough of listening to her self-pity!'

We hear things like this almost every day.

Whether it's a witty exchange or a deep conversation, the best part of communicating with someone is the natural back-and-forth – like a game of catch. But with email and texting the primary means of communication in both work and life, we lose out on seeing each other's faces and creating an in-the-moment rhythm, and the things we want to say get bottled up inside.

So it's understandable that people will occasionally want to release some of their pent-up grievances – doing so can help to alleviate stress.

What the person doing the complaining will most appreciate in this case is a skilled listener. While they are pouring their heart out, if the other person makes a blatantly unpleasant face as if to say, 'More complaints?' or if it's obvious that they aren't listening attentively, it could have the opposite effect of adding to their stress instead of lightening it. It might actually drive them towards self-loathing.

The thing you have to grasp as a listener – aside from being considerate enough not to interrupt the conversation or impede its flow – is that you're there to validate what the other person has to say, to offer your opinion in exchange, and to sympathize with them.

'If someone had said that to me, I probably would have lost it.'

'I get it. It's only natural to be angry about that.'

Responses like this signal your sympathy, and when you make it clear that you're listening to them, the other person won't feel as if their complaint is unjustified. It ends up being a major stress reliever.

Of course, the other person shouldn't hesitate to return the favour to such an excellent listener. The next time you feel like grumbling, they should be the one to listen with the same attentiveness.

This give-and-take is the secret to making relationships work. Allowing each other to voice your complaints when you need to helps the relationship develop and deepen.

There is the Zen phrase, 'The cool breeze sweeps away the bright moonlight, the bright moonlight clears away the cool breeze.'

While both the cool breeze and the bright moonlight are beautiful, they each take their turn, and together heighten the beauty of the whole.

If we apply this to human relationships, we could say that one friend leans on the other, who then supports them. Each person relying on the other when most needed fosters the trust that leads to deep connection.

Indeed, the bond between two people grows stronger when each feels they've been heard.

I've mentioned Buddhism's Seven Gifts of Spiritual Dana, as they are called, which are a practice of gifts we can offer to others.

One of the dana is 'kind heart'.

Kind heart means sympathizing with others. Devoting time to listening to someone's problems – this is undoubtedly a sympathetic gesture. What if you were to take the opportunity to practise giving this gift to others. The practice of these gifts is an important part of Zen training, because listening to what troubles others can be a way of honing your own heart – it helps to deepen your generosity as a human being.

40. DON'T BASE DECISIONS ON PROFITS AND LOSSES

Relationships that aren't based on personal gain
will shine of their own accord

In life, there are various milestones and crossroads.

At these points, we might lose our way, or be plagued by worries and doubts.

They force us to make choices. And we need a set of criteria in order to decide what to do. Naturally, these are related to our values.

For instance, when you look for a job, you'll consider the nature of the work, the salary, benefits, vacation time, how demanding the work is, what kind of status it confers, the location of the office, among other things, and you'll weigh the advantages against the disadvantages, or the profits against the losses.

Such standards of profit and loss play into relationships as well. We calculate advantages and disadvantages when we get to know people. It might look like this:

'I happened to meet this guy – he works for XX company – they're a big client of ours, aren't they? I definitely need to get to know him better. I'll give him a call first thing tomorrow.'

'Oh, she's just a subcontractor, right? Well, then, I don't need to bother getting to know her.'

You might cultivate certain relationships because they're helpful or advantageous to you, or brush someone off because you decide there's nothing in it for you.

Outside of work, too, you might try to please that person who generously picks up the cheque while being dismissive of the one who you figure has no advantage to offer.

Of course, I realize that the world is not made up only of idealists, and that no matter who you are, a bit of calculation comes into play.

However, we mustn't base our relationships on expediency.

If you seek out someone because it seems important for you to do so, it will end poorly. Not wanting to offend them or get on their bad side, you'll always be grovelling or flattering, and you'll become obsequious.

The relationship will be imbalanced, with the other person dominant and you subordinate.

And amid all this, your spirit will dim. Your energy will flag. You'll lose your spark. You'll lose confidence.

We have a saying in Zen, 'The supreme way knows no difficulty, only avoid picking and choosing.'

The supreme way refers to the path to enlightenment. We imagine that in order to reach enlightenment, we must follow very austere training and practice, but that is not true. The path to enlightenment is by no means difficult. But the one thing we mustn't do is make decisions based on calculation and the weighing of all possibilities – we simply cannot be selective. That is the meaning of this Zen phrase.

Everyone thinks that the way to enlightenment is by living a beatific life, a life of happiness. But going through life like this requires us to stop assessing – we must not be so particular.

Weighing profits and losses is a prime example of this.

While you are busy evaluating everything, you will be not be able to form relationships with truly good people. You will be unable to live a good life, unable to create a bright and happy path for yourself.

There is another Zen expression, 'Hogejaku', which means, 'Let go of everything.'

Surely the first thing we should let go of is a preoccupation with profits and losses.

When we let go of this, then we can see more clearly the important things in life.

part five

Change *how* you worry about things
and your life will change for the better

On money, aging, illness, death, and more

41. MONEY

The desire for more only makes everything harder

These are the Buddha's words:

'Human desire is such that, even if the Himalayas were turned to gold, it would not be enough.'

Human desire is boundless. There is no limit to it.

The classic manifestation of desire is money.

There is no end to our pursuit of it. If there is something we want, we save our money in order to acquire it. But once we acquire it, we soon want something else or something better. And so we desire more and more money.

Ultimately, even when there is nothing in particular that we want, we still find ourselves in pursuit of money. We are constrained by it, driven by it. It's hardly a way to be free.

Life can be seen as being about doing what we want, working hard at what we're good at, and making some kind of contribution to society. And we can make some money for doing that.

But we do not live for money. We live to work hard at what we want and to contribute to society, not to amass money. It is when these things are reversed that I think life feels empty.

There is the phrase, 'Desire little and know contentment.' In the Bequeathed Teachings Sutra that the Buddha offered on his deathbed, here is what he said about desiring little and knowing contentment:

'Those who know satisfaction, even when lying on the ground, are still comfortable and at ease. Those who do not know satisfaction, even when living in a palace, are still not sated. Those who do not know satisfaction, even if rich, are poor.'

If you live your life thinking, 'I have plenty, I am grateful,' even if your home is modest and your meals simple, then you will be rich in spirit. But if you live your life thinking, 'I will never be satisfied with what I have,' even if you live in a mansion and indulge in extravagant meals, then your spirit will remain parched.

You can buy all the brand-name items you want, but you will never be satisfied. When the next new one comes out, you will be distracted by the need to have it – some people even to the point of committing a crime for it. This can become a miserable existence.

If you pay no attention to brands, you will be satisfied with only the things that please you, and when you use them well, you will grow even more fond of them, and you won't be distracted by all the products competing for your attention.

The Japanese have a maxim: 'When awake, half a mat; when asleep, one mat; even if you rule the world, four to five bowls.'

No matter how great you are, when you're awake, all the space you need is half a tatami mat; when you're asleep, a full tatami mat; and no matter how much status and influence you may have, all you need for one meal is four to five small bowls.

Basically, that is all there is to human existence.

So, will you be one who knows satisfaction, or one who can never be satisfied?

Which path will you choose?

42. GETTING OLDER

The more you're able to forgive, the happier you'll be

'Lately, my physical strength seems diminished . . .'

'I have less energy now than I used to . . .'

As we age, we may, like trees, accumulate more growth rings, so to speak, but that doesn't necessarily mean that there is a corresponding increase in our satisfaction with life.

In fact, once people approach retirement age, they often experience a sense of emptiness.

What tends to happen is that they stop doing things, they spend all day watching television, they become much less active.

Some time ago, a phrase caught on that poked fun at certain husbands who had retired from work, referring to them as 'wet fallen leaves'. Once corporate warriors, they now cling to their wives like leaves on the ground that, when wet, seem impossible to dislodge.

Aging can be difficult. But retiring from work doesn't mean that you retire from life.

Instead of lamenting how old you are, why not set out to discover the benefits that come with aging?

When you live a long life, you accumulate a wealth of experiences that enrich your life and often equip you to persevere through hardship and struggle.

Each of these experiences trains your mind, making you a more generous spirit. Things that you wouldn't have tolerated in the prime of your life can now be dismissed with an attitude of 'Well, these things happen.' Ways of thinking that had been difficult to accept now become easier to take in your stride – 'I see, that's one way to think about it.' With this generous spirit, you can't help but open yourself to more experiences, which may be one of the greatest gifts of aging.

There is a Zen saying that comes from Goto Egen, a historiography of the Zen sect established in the Southern Song Dynasty period in China. The meaning is this: as we grow weak with age, we grow languid as well; we are no longer attached to this transient world; without any obsessions or concerns, we have no greater pleasure than to admire the verdant hills as we lie in repose.

This is the epitome of a generous spirit. As we age, we might feel frustrated or anxious because we are nostalgic about our lost youth. But no matter how we resist, there's nothing we can do about it. We must simply accept aging, and adopt a relaxed attitude.

The author Seiko Tanabe has this to say:

'Isn't learning more about people one of the pleasures of aging?'

With a wealth of experience and knowledge, it can be a pleasure to observe younger generations. Let's awaken that generosity of spirit.

43. OLD AGE

Zen teachings for maintaining your appearance,
your posture, your breathing . . .

— · — · — · — · —

I often say, 'It's important to be philosophical about old age.'

But being philosophical about it isn't the same as surrendering to it.

Take your appearance and grooming, for one. Some people may spend most of their time at home and favour a tracksuit. But this is better than wearing their pyjamas, and they may put on something different when they run out to the shops.

Our appearance has an influence on our spirit. When we present ourselves neatly and tidily, we stand up a little straighter. When we stand up straight, our chest expands and we breathe more deeply, which also gives us more mental energy.

Another thing to consider as we get on in years is the value of developing a sense of humour. Humour can relieve tension and cheer people up. It also acts as a social lubricant.

You need a supple mind in order to sprinkle humour into your conversations. It encourages you to keep up with what's going on in the world and helps you to maintain a fresh perspective.

When Danshi Tatekawa, the famous rakugo comic storyteller, was young, he had gone to the beach with another rakugo master, the late Enraku Sanyutei. Tatekawa-san happened to look out at the sea and see that Enraku-san was far from shore and in danger of drowning. But instead of trying to rescue him, apparently Tatekawa-san just sat there, calmly watching Enraku-san drown.

Someone else came to Enraku-san's rescue and, not surprisingly, he then reproached Tatekawa-san. 'Why didn't you try to help me?' he asked. It is said that Tatekawa-san responded nonchalantly, 'If both of us were to die, that'd have been the end of the rakugo world. I figured if at least I survived, it might be saved.'

Imagining this scene, don't you find that your lips relax and curl into a smile? The mood softens, doesn't it?

Humour has extraordinary power.

As I've said, the essence of Zen is practice. So don't be afraid of being ridiculed for making 'dad jokes' – just start reeling off your own attempts at humour.

44. LOVE

Even in matters of love, moderation is just right

Whatever I have to say about love might be embarrassing, but I will pluck up my courage and try to express my thoughts on the subject.

In love, the thing to keep in mind is the Confucian teaching of 'Hara hachi bun me' or 'Belly eight parts full', which means that we should eat until we are eighty per cent full.

Here's what I mean by invoking 'Belly eight parts full' here.

'Don't expect your partner to be per fect.'

When we are in the throes of love, we do everything we can to try to identify with our partner.

We want them to know one hundred per cent of the things about us, and likewise we want to know one hundred per cent of the things about them. However, the possibility of knowing everything there is to know about a fellow human being – where they were born, the environment they grew up in, the education they received, the people they've been involved with – and comprehending it all is impossible.

Obviously, we're all different. We must not forget this. If you and your partner can understand eighty per cent about each other – that is to say, if you can accept that eighty per cent is enough – it is likely to be good for your relationship, and to enable you to strike the right balance.

Twenty per cent of your partner will remain 'uncharted territory'. The mystery and intrigue of it will sustain your interest in (and affection for) them.

There's no such thing as one hundred per cent mutual understanding, and even if there were, wouldn't the freshness and attraction you felt when you first met fade?

If you understand only fifty per cent about your partner, it seems to me that a relationship would be difficult. 'He's so different to me,' you might often find yourself saying.

Appearance is a key factor at the beginning of a relationship. What first draws you to someone is that you think they're cute, or attractive, or handsome, or pretty.

Whatever it is, though, that brings you together, once you realize how your values differ, it's a good idea to take a pause. Otherwise, if you decide to get married based solely on your first impressions, your differences in values could produce cracks or fissures in your relationship.

Take attitudes about money, for instance – one of you may be the type who saves money and spends it cautiously, while the other may, as the saying goes, spend the day's earnings before the day is done.

If you manage to keep an open mind, at first you will probably tolerate the difference, but your patience won't last forever. Before long, your attitudes will collide, and you may be headed for a break-up.

It's the same for time management. If someone who enjoys spending their leisure time relaxing and listening to music or reading books is living with someone who prefers to use their leisure time being out and about, going shopping, and eating at restaurants, it's a foregone conclusion that there will be friction.

Or take eating: if one person loves calorie-laden foods that are high-in-fat, while the other likes simple and fresh meals, it's unlikely they're going to be able to enjoy many meals together.

'Love is beautiful misunderstanding, marriage is cruel understanding.' If in the whirl of love you can remember the eighty-per cent rule of 'Belly eight parts full,' you can prove the adage wrong.

45. MARRIAGE

Words of appreciation make a good relationship

— — — — —

Between couples who have been married a long time, there tends to be less and less to talk about. Each partner may even begin to regard the other's existence almost as part of the air around them, especially when there's nothing in particular that needs to be communicated. Like in those lonely days of yore, when the only three words a husband would utter inside the house were 'bath', 'dinner', and 'bed', you can practically hear the wind blowing through the cracks in the drafty marriage.

Here's what one wife has to say:

'There's plenty of talking in my house, even if most of it is complaining. His boss said this, his client did that . . . I know that for him, talking about work is a way to relieve stress, but for me who always, always has to listen to it – it adds up, you know!'

I think she makes a valid point. Maybe it still holds true for her that 'It's best if the husband is healthy but out of the house.'

But think about it a bit more. What does it mean if your spouse complains a lot? It's not as if the husband can complain

to just anyone – for example, he can't say these things at the office, can he?

Even if he does have someone at the office to complain to, doing so could be risky. Or the person he's complaining to might say, 'I don't want to hear any more – if you're so unhappy, why don't you quit?' The prevailing image of a husband outside the home is that he grins and bears it, no matter how much he keeps bottled up inside.

Being the one whom your partner can complain to shows that you're trusted. It amounts to a declaration that they feel comfortable baring their heart to you, and that they feel secure enough to do so. With this in mind, perhaps it won't bother you as much?

We have a word in Zen – 'ro' – that refers to being completely exposed or unprotected, with nothing hidden. In the world of the tea ceremony, which is deeply connected with Zen, the open ground of the garden that surrounds the teahouse is called the 'roji'.

The roji is a space that allows us to be our true self. As we walk towards the teahouse, we lay bare our nature. It used to be that people were born into or held various ranks or standings within society, such as samurai, poet, merchant . . . and for each of these, they were required to wear the appropriate armour for their station.

The purpose of the roji is to serve as a place that says, 'Please, enter here and cast aside that which clings to you.'

Having cast off the things that cling to you, your original nature is revealed, and as you enter the teahouse that represents a Buddha realm, you cross the boundaries of rank or standing with an open heart . . . This is the world of 'chanoyu', the Way of Tea envisioned by the great tea master Sen no Rikyu.

Complaining would seem to be very different from the Way of Tea, but like the Way of Tea, it is about baring and giving voice to your true nature, allowing you to express trust in your partner in a burst of candid feelings. It would be unfortunate to respond with 'Here he goes again!'

To be sure, complaining is a tacit expression of trust, one that must be inferred by the listener. It's better to convey trust more explicitly and openly.

You might come home with a sullen look on your face, and neither you nor your partner says a word to each other as you watch television before going to bed. But if you announce 'I'm home!' when you walk in the door, then your partner can come to welcome you and ask how your day was.

Zen is about action and behaviour. It's not good enough just to feel comfortable trusting someone – it is important to try to act in a way that conveys your trust.

One way to do this would be to express your gratitude with a 'thank-you' when someone serves you a meal or a beverage. Or when a larger-than-usual shopping trip is required, a bit of consultation before the outing and even an offer to assist can demonstrate thoughtfulness. Now is the time to start creating an environment in which you can openly express your complaints, by making your partner aware that you're doing so because they have your confidence and trust, for which you are grateful.

46. CHILDREN

Helicopter parenting plants seeds of worry

So much about the parent-child relationship has changed over the years.

Perhaps the biggest shift is in whether to be 'hands-on'. In the past, families had many children and households were poorer, so parents weren't able to be very involved with their children.

It wasn't unusual for the oldest brother or sister to mind the younger siblings, looking after them and taking care of them in various ways.

Children had some distance from their parents, which enabled them to achieve their independence. What's more, the tumult of sibling relationships imparted critical knowledge of the Confucian hierarchical social order among older and younger members, and encouraged consideration towards those weaker than you.

With the decline in the birth rate, parents can be increasingly hands-on with their children.

And with the intense competition, almost from birth, to position children for educational success, it seems that if you are a good son or daughter, especially one who studies hard, it's not particularly unusual for your parents to do everything for you.

Unable to make and act upon their own decisions, always awaiting instructions before making a move . . . there's no doubt that this tendency of today's young people stems from this infantilizing parent-child dynamic.

Here is an amazing story, a strange incident that occurred at
a police department just south of Tokyo:

The new chief of police arrived to assume his post, and the
department staff gathered to welcome him. The new chief's
mother was standing in front, just as the chief was about to give
his first remarks. She grabbed the microphone, paying no
attention to the man of the hour, and proceeded to give a
speech about her son. Imagine how stunned the police
department staff was.

A mother is a mother and a son is a son. Even if a mother cannot
let her child go out on his own, even if she always insists on
going with him, shouldn't she still have enough common sense
to know how inappropriate this was? And wouldn't it have been
reasonable for the son to say, 'What are you thinking?' and to
claim his authority? That such an accomplished individual did
not do so, that he behaved as a little boy in front of dozens or
even hundreds of police officers, almost defies belief.

Of course, I don't mean to imply that this is typical,
but I wouldn't be surprised if this kind of thing has
occurred elsewhere.

Helicopter parenting only intensifies the problem. It spoils
the child.

In Buddhism, there are what we call the 'three poisons' – greed, anger and ignorance – which represent the worldly temptations that we must overcome. Another way is to think of them, respectively, as 'a covetous heart', 'a rageful heart', and 'a foolish heart'.

Helicopter parenting is toxic – an expression of ignorance.

Buddhism has these words to offer: 'To think that you have wealth because you have a child is what brings suffering upon the foolish. We do not own even our own selves, so how can we own a child or wealth?'

If you can rid your mind of the foolish idea that you own your children, then you will enjoy a refreshing, proper and happy relationship with them.

47. DEATH

We should entrust our dying to the Buddha

As we advance in age, we may not like to admit that death comes closer to being a reality. We might feel this most acutely when we approach the ages our parents were when they passed away.

Up until then, we likely have attended funerals for the parents of friends, acquaintances and work colleagues, and the words of mourning we expressed were meaningful at the time, but I suspect we did not keenly feel the looming spectre of death.

'I'd been to several funerals, where I'd offered my condolences, but I never really understood what it was like for the grieving family. It wasn't until the death of one of my parents that I came to know what it's like to lose someone important to you.'

I often hear this kind of thing. Death feels real when one of your parents passes away, and the age of their death becomes a marker for your life as well.

'Ah, the life that's left is like spare change.'

This is indeed how it was for my father. The ages at which his parents died became a marker, and he lived his life to the fullest up to that point, but beyond that, I think, he gratefully accepted the remaining time as 'spare change'.

When we ourselves have reached the age at which our parents passed away, we may think, 'Ah, soon it will be the New Year's Eve of my own life.'

The *Shushogi* – 'the meaning of practice and verification' – is a text of important extracts from Dogen Zenji's *Shogobenzo*, intended to make the tenets of Soto Zen Buddhism easier for laypeople to understand. It has five sections, each with thirty-one paragraphs. The first section begins with the following:

'The most important issue of all for Buddhists is the thorough clarification of the meaning of birth and death.'

Dogen Zenji also said, 'When we are alive, we must live completely. When we die, we must die completely.'

Why does Zen always complicate things, you may ask? But this is not all that difficult, really. While we are alive, thinking about death creates anxiety and fear. This is because we conceive of death as the end of life, an extinguishing of it.

There is a Zen expression, 'Do not judge the past or future.'

Each moment exists unto itself, with no relationship to that which came before it or that which comes after it. Life and death are each their own absolute. Life is not about moving towards death, and death is not about being the end of life.

To live completely is to fulfill the absolute of this life by living it to the best of your ability. Since we have no control over our own death, we should entrust it to the Buddha. If we live completely, the absolute of death will naturally follow. That is how to die completely . . . I think this is what Dogen Zenji meant.

While you are alive, dedicate yourself only to living.

There is no anxiety or fear of death inherent in doing that.

Earlier I referred to Ekiho Miyazaki, who lived to be 106 and even past the age of 100 maintained the same ascetic practices as those of young monks. He said this:

'People ask themselves when is a good time to die, and they think, After I'm enlightened. But that's wrong. To live peacefully and with composure, that is enlightenment. It isn't difficult to live peacefully and with composure. When it comes time to die, it's best to die. While it's time to live, it's best to live peacefully and with composure.'

To me, Miyazaki Zenji's idea of living 'peacefully and with composure' is the same as Dogen Zenji's idea that 'we must live completely.'

There is no doubt that this is indeed difficult, but it is the state we should aspire to. Beyond it lies the serenity of the absolute of death.

48. ONE'S END

What words will you be remembered by?

– – – – –

As you prepare to meet your end, what are the words you would like to be remembered by?

At the time of his death, one of my parishioners chose to leave us with 'Banzai!' This one word, which means eternal life and prosperity, summed up everything he had accomplished in life, and a lifetime in which he had not left anything behind.

But this simply won't do. It is said that the last words of the famous monk and head priest Sengai, who lived during Japan's Edo period (1603–1868), were, 'I will not go with death.' Sengai was known for his lack of inhibition. He once composed a satirical poem brimming with sarcasm about the government of the daimyo's chief retainer:

'It will not end well for the retainer who thinks all is well. The previous retainer thought all was well.'

So Sengai's disciples did not know whether to take his last words at face value. I myself wonder if there wasn't some deeper meaning to them.

It was customary for Zen monks, at the beginning of each year, to practise composing yuige, death poems in Chinese verse that reflected their state of mind. This tradition has faded, but I imagine that some of the yuige may ultimately have served as the monks' final words.

My own father left behind a yuige:

Clear ground where the weeds are gone, grass makes way
for the pure land

These eight-seven years, these eight-seven years

Exhausting my health, merely to serve at Kenko

Shiho intended, in Zen, to walk the path in faith, towards
tranquillity and peace

He incorporated his own name, Shiho, as well as the name of the temple where he served as head priest, Kenkoji, into this poem. I can't help but think that the feelings my father had about his life are reflected in his yuige.

I encourage you to consider writing down your own feelings about your state of mind at the start of the new year. Of course, it's not necessary that these include an awareness of death. They can be about your resolutions – what your hopes are for the year to come, how you would like to live out the new year. Whatever thoughts come up for you as you turn the calendar.

Here's another option. Every year on 12 December, there is a ceremony at Kiyomizu Temple in Kyoto in which they announce the 'Kanji of the Year', the character that has been voted as representative of the previous year. At the beginning of the year, you might choose a word that represents your mental state at that moment.

We don't know when death will happen, but as long as we are human, it will come to all of us. When that time arrives, what the loved ones who are left behind will most want to know is what were the feelings of their dearly departed.

'Ah, is this what they were thinking about, is this what they felt?'

If we could get just a glimpse of what those we've lost were thinking, gleaned from what they wrote down at the beginning of the year, it would be that much easier to send them off in our hearts. That's how I feel about it.

Consider making your own yuige an annual tradition.

INDEX OF ZENGO, OR ZEN SAYINGS

Look carefully at what is under your own feet.
(Foreword, page 10)

Eat and drink with your whole heart.
(Foreword, page 11)

Delude not thyself.
(Chapter 1, page 14)

Once enlightened, there are no favourites.
(Chapter 1, page 16)

Dwell in the breath.
(Chapter 2, page 18)

Walking hand-in-hand.
(Chapter 4, page 29)

Don't wear coloured glasses.
(Chapter 6, page 36)

For every seven times you run, you should sit once.
(Chapter 10, page 51)

Spiritual enlightenment comes only through personal experience. (Chapter 13, page 66)

Change the great earth into gold.
(Chapter 15, page 74)

The cloud is egoless, it is not undone by the ravine.
(Chapter 16, page 78)

Even when the eight winds blow, do not be moved.
(Chapter 18, page 88)

The old awl comes in handy.
(Chapter 22, page 102)

Every day is a good day.
(Chapter 23, page 106)

All things come from nothingness.
(Chapter 25, page 112)

A flexible mind.
(Chapter 27, page 120)

Enlightenment is not dependent on words
or writing, and spiritual awakening can be attained
only through intuitive discernment.
(Chapter 28, page 122)

The ordinary mind is the way.
(Chapter 29, page 126)

Return home and sit at ease.
(Chapter 30, page 132)

Ichi-go ichi-e: Once in a lifetime.
(Chapter 31, page 138)

Every step is a place to learn.
(Chapter 32, page 142)

Gentle face, loving words.
(Chapter 33, page 146)

When you see a flower, savour the flower, and
when you see the moon, savour the moon.
(Chapter 35, page 154)

Menju: face-to-face.
(Chapter 37, page 162)

Open the gate and you will find long life and happiness.
(Chapter 38, page 164)

The cool breeze sweeps away the bright moonlight, the bright
moonlight clears away the cool breeze.
(Chapter 39, page 168)

The supreme way knows no difficulty,
only avoid picking and choosing.
(Chapter 40, page 172)

Hogejaku: let go of everything.
(Chapter 40, page 173)

Do not judge the past or future.
(Chapter 47, page 198)

MICHAEL JOSEPH

UK | USA | Canada | Ireland | Australia
India | New Zealand | South Africa

Michael Joseph is part of the Penguin Random House group of companies
whose addresses can be found at global.penguinrandomhouse.com

Penguin
Random House
UK

First published in the United States of America by Penguin Books 2022
First published in Great Britain by Michael Joseph 2022

Originally published in Japanese as *Shinpaigoto no Kyuwari wa Okoranai* by
Mikasa-Shobo Publishers Co., Ltd., Tokyo

This edition published by arrangement with Penguin Books, an imprint of Penguin
Publishing Group, a division of Penguin Random House LLC and in conjunction
with Mikasa-Shobo Publishers Co., Ltd., Tokyo c/o Tuttle-Mori Agency, Inc., Tokyo

003

Copyright © Shunmyō Masuno, 2022
Translation copyright © Allison Markin Powell, for the English language translation
Illustration copyright © Zanna and Harry Goldhawk, 2022

The moral right of the author and translator has been asserted

Set in Bembo and Futura.
Printed in Italy by Printer Trento S.r.l.

The authorized representative in the EEA is Penguin Random House Ireland,
Morrison Chambers, 32 Nassau Street, Dublin D02 YH68

A CIP catalogue record for this book is available
from the British Library

ISBN: 978–0–241–55182–0

www.greenpenguin.co.uk